TRAINING FOR DE

Also by John Adair:

HASTINGS TO CULLODEN (*co-author*)
TRAINING FOR LEADERSHIP
ROUNDHEAD GENERAL: A military
biography of Sir William Waller

TRAINING FOR DECISIONS

JOHN ADAIR

MACDONALD : LONDON

To
Bernard Babington Smith

CONTENTS

	Preface	9
1	The Nature of Thinking	13
2	Thinkers in Action	26
3	Decision Making	49
4	Sharing Decisions	65
5	Problem Solving	79
6	Creative Thinking	90
7	Decisions about People	101
8	Experiments in Training	109
9	Training for Decisions	125
	Conclusion	139
	Appendix 1 Some Techniques for Managers	142
	Appendix 2 Puzzle Problems	148
	Appendix 3 Problem Solving Exercise : The Paint Spray Gun	150
	Notes and Bibliography	154
	Index	163

PREFACE

'Decision making', 'problem solving' and 'creative thinking' : these three topics have attracted considerable attention in recent years, not only from those with an academic interest in them but also from men and women in all walks of life whose work directly involves these mental activities and who want to improve their daily performance of them. In particular, managers in industry, commerce and the public services throughout the world have created a demand for seminars, courses, books and articles on these topics and there are no signs that their interest is falling away. What may happen, however, is that they become daunted or confused by the sheer variety of courses and the wealth of literature on these matters. For example, the current British Institute of Management select reading lists on 'creative thinking' and 'problem solving' contains thirty-six books and eighteen articles in periodicals, while 'decision making' musters no less than forty-seven book titles and thirty-two articles. In both lists only six publications are dated before 1960.

The first aim of this book is to provoke thought and discussion about what could be called the mental or intellectual dimension of leadership in any sphere of life. For all leaders in organizations must make decisions and also help others to arrive at them as well.

My second aim, however, is to attempt to introduce some order or system into the profusion of literature, training approaches, claims and counter-claims which we have inherited from the past in an area of management studies which most people recognize to be of first importance.

Thirdly, I have suggested a possible outline for a short seminar in decision making, problem solving and creative thinking, based upon a clearer understanding of the nature of thinking, and draw-

9

ing upon some of the better methods at present available in this field and tested in trial training sessions with managers of all levels.

It may disappoint some readers that this book does not contain more mathematics; most books today with the word 'decision' in their titles turn out to be full of graphs, sums and equations. My own point of view is that mathematics do have an important part to play in managerial decisions, especially those which involve choosing the best means towards a given end, but that it is not the chief or leading role. To some extent I hope this book will restore a balance which has become weighted towards those who are coming to see all managerial decisions in terms of mathematics, often based upon highly speculative assumptions. The artificial intelligence of computers is most useful, but it is not a substitute for human judgement.

The book begins with an exploration of the ways in which human thought bears the fruits of right decisions. Without a greater degree of clarity on how the mind works in purposeful activity we shall not be able to improve our methods of training and educating it for its essential work, and so I make no apology for this excursion into the world of the mind. With the 'case studies' in Chapter Two the reader has the opportunity of relating or applying the outline general model or theory of thinking presented in the first chapter to concrete situations or people : it is the dialogue between theory and practice which leads us forward.

From the unifying or integrating theme of Chapter One the book unfolds naturally. Decision making, problem solving, creative thinking and judgements about people are all explored in turn. The increasing importance of participation in decisions is also considered in a chapter entitled 'Sharing Decisions'. But the book is not designed to study in any detail the implementation of decisions in organizations once they are irrevocably made. The focus is much more on the intellectual, psychological and social processes of actually reaching the best possible decision in a given situation.

In the last section various training methods and courses are reviewed in the light of their underlying philosophy or assumptions. All have contributions to make but none is satisfactory in isolation. The description of a design for a short course concludes the book. Its presence within these covers serves to emphasize the fundamentally practical concern of this study : the theoretical or academic is eschewed unless it seems to have some practical relevance to the thinking or training of leaders in all the varied working situations of our industrial society.

May I add that the word 'training' in the title is meant to embrace 'self-training'. Like leadership itself, no one can *teach* us how to think or decide better – we can only *learn* to do so ourselves with the help of others. This book is offered primarily to those who wish to extend the reach of their own minds and only secondly to those who are responsible for developing the intellectual potential of practical decision makers. At the very least its tentative conclusions will offer plenty of practice for those who wish to exercise their critical faculties, but I trust that these pages will also stimulate other fruitful lines of thought and action.

Some of the topics of this book I have discussed with Bernard Babington Smith, Senior Lecturer in Experimental Psychology at the University of Oxford, to whom this book is dedicated. In particular, I owe to him the invaluable distinction between purpose, aims and objectives which I have developed in Chapter Three. Also I am deeply grateful to Professor Sir Lawrence Bragg FRS for giving me his permission to make use of the television profile of him in Chapter Two, and to the British Broadcasting Corporation for supplying the script. My friends and colleagues have as always been generous with their time in commenting on various drafts : in this respect I should especially like to thank Lady Margaret Brown, Miss Elizabeth Andrews and David Charles-Edwards. Professors John Cohen and Liam Hudson have kindly answered queries from me, and Mr Jerry Rhodes, the managing director of Kepner-Tregoe Ltd in the United Kingdom, gave generously of his time to comment upon and discuss my description of the particular training approach and methods associated with his firm, for which assistance I am most thankful. Last but not least, I owe an immense debt to all those managers with whom I have worked in applying the general ideas in this book to the particular requirements for decision making, problem solving and creative thinking which face them as leaders in industry, commerce and the public services.

CHAPTER ONE

THE NATURE OF THINKING

Thinking about thinking is naturally a difficult business, indeed some think it an impossible one, like trying to jump on your own shadow. It may also seem a rather distasteful occupation. For many people do not care to analyse such a living process as thought : they recoil from the necessary introversion. They fear that the whole movement and colour of their minds will be dissected and explained in psychological or chemical terms.

On the other hand, to be practical, all of us do have to spend much of our time thinking in the deliberate or conscious sense of that word. We have to formulate problems, consider alternatives, search for new ones and choose courses of action. Depending on the matter a decision may be almost instant or it may take years of reflection and inquiry. Increasingly we tend to be selected for our jobs, judged and paid by our capacity to make the right decision. Sometimes that decision may be only a careful choice between known possibilities. More often than not, however, in a rapidly changing society, it will require a creative dimension, the bringing in of the unexpected into a familiar situation.

For this reason among others I do not believe that one can divide thought into separate categories such as logical and creative thinking, or usefully maintain for long distinctions between problem solving or decision making or creativity. The intellect is a whole, a unity which resists such division. In calling this book *Training for Decisions* I am using the last word as a part to describe a whole. Most deliberate thinking is walking around the base of a decision, or pushing on slowly up its lower slopes or going over the summit and then viewing it from the other side. A decision does not end the process of thinking – it is just one peak in a range of mountains that may show itself more clearly above the clouds.

Before getting involved with all the intellectual detail described and discussed in the 'how-to-do-it' books, articles and courses, let us therefore first take a step back, so to speak, and look at thinking itself. For it may well be that many of the confusions and contradictions evident in the writings and teachings on these interrelated subjects spring from treating them as separate or autonomous too early on.

Certainly if we look at these well-worn phrases the only concept common to all of them is thinking. 'Problem' comes from a Greek word meaning literally a thing thrown or put forward, and is mainly defined as a 'a doubtful or difficult question; a matter of inquiry, discussion or thought', while 'solving' springs from the Latin *solvere*, to loosen or break, which came to mean : 'explaining, clearing up, resolving or answering'. The *Shorter Oxford English Dictionary* also defines 'to decide' as : 'to determine (a question, controversy or cause) by giving the victory to one side or other; to settle, resolve'. Thinking is obviously implied by the phrase creative thinking although the stress often seems to be placed on the first word, with its overtones of effortless inspiration, rather than the second.

However, when we turn for information to the psychologists about the more shadowy process of thinking behind the more definite or concrete terms mentioned above they have little to tell us, at least not in a form made coherent by any general theory. 'We know very little about the psychology of thinking', wrote Robert Thompson in *The Psychology of Thinking* (1959). 'The psychologist cannot claim to be able to offer a complete description or a well-evidenced general theory to explain how we come to think the way we do. This book gives an interim report on what the psychologists have had to say on the subject so far.'[1]

Evolution and thinking

The elaboration of a general theory concerning the origins of thinking, or 'how we have come to think the way we do', is beyond the scope of this present book, which has the improvement of practical or applied thinking as its aim. Yet if the first step towards any advance in education or training is an increase in awareness and if one part of the latter springs from a knowledge of origins and development – in short the historical approach – then a brief introduction to a general theory about the beginnings and therefore (to some degree) the nature of thinking is certainly relevant.

Perhaps an understanding of how we have come to think the way we do can be gained best in the context of the general theory of evolution. If the process of evolution has become conscious in man, as many distinguished scientists have argued,[2] may not thinking have its roots in the unconscious and (gradually) conscious response of man to the challenges of his environment?

Essentially the theory of evolution rests on the assumption that life in all its forms is a precarious state of matter always striving to maintain its existence, and suggests that changes in a biological species take place as result of responses to the challenges posed to it by the environment. The method of evolutionary adaption is 'natural selection' : a complex process by which information from the environment influences the ever-changing pattern of genetic mutations in the species to adapt it to the conditions in which it finds itself. Let us now explore what happens when this pattern of environment–information–change becomes conscious in the mind of man. The main suggestion in this chapter is that thinking in the deliberate or purposeful sense of the word takes three basic forms, all related to the evolutionary advance of man, namely : analysing, synthesizing, and valuing.

Analysing

If the process of response was to become conscious it would imply some sort of analysis of the information received from the environment. 'Analysis' is a key word and to be used often in this book, and therefore it needs a definition. The *Shorter Oxford English Dictionary* derives it from the Greek verb 'to loosen', and gives the primary meaning as 'resolution into simple parts'. In other words, when I take my watch to pieces I can strictly be said to be analysing it. The word, however, has overtones of meaning beyond this simple physical act of taking things apart. Indeed, the concept of 'loosening' does not imply a complete separation of elements. The knot tying two pieces of rope may be untied, or merely loosened, so that the nature of the knot can be understood. Analysis implies the tracing of things to their sources, and the discovery of general principles underlying concrete phenomena.

In the context of evolution man's superior ability as an analyst of his environment has clearly aided his continued survival. By separating and categorizing sense data, by probing behind the surface of appearances to unseen or abstract general principles, man has increased his control over the environment. Curiosity, therefore, or man's inherent inquisitiveness, had a survival value : the roots of our present desire to learn or know may thus lie far back in the ancestral era of *homo sapiens*. The child pulling a toy to pieces to find out how it works is father to the man.

We are, however, endowed with a much greater desire to analyse than is required for our physical survival. As in other spheres nature seems to strive for success by its sheer prodigality and tolerance for immense waste. Many of our intellectual analysing activities are no longer means, however far removed, towards survival ends; they have become exercises for their own sake. In other words we analyse because we have the capacity to do it, regardless of the environment's challenges. Our culture and civilization are partly results of this 'over-plus' of analytical ability.

Reinforcing the exercise of our inherent analytical talent lies the fact that we like doing it : there is a pleasure in successful analysis. Despite the popular notion of a dichotomy between thinking and feeling, between cold reason and warm emotion, nature has reinforced the total activity of thinking by a whole range of emotions. We feel baffled before an apparently intractable problem, elated at its elucidation : witness the famous story of Archimedes leaping from his bath and running through the streets shouting, 'Eureka! Eureka!' There is a pleasure to be found in loosening or separating a whole into its constituent parts, tracing its origins or discerning an underlying theory or principle, the relation of the parts to the whole. The common experience of understanding can come to us as a relief from the pain of incomprehension, the delight of a conquest after a costly struggle. 'If you had two lives that would not be enough for you,' declared the Russian scientist Pavlov in his *Bequest to Academic Youth*. 'Be passionate in your work and your searchings.'[3]

Synthesizing

A second strand or theme in thinking is 'synthesis'. Again this word comes from the Greek language, and it means the opposite of analysing, namely : 'the putting together of parts or elements so as to make up a complex whole'. Indeed the Latin verb *cogito*, 'I think', can be derived from roots meaning 'to shake together'. When the resulting whole is substantially original we can describe the synthetic process as creative. There is a sense in which all syntheses are new, and it is a pity to restrict the word creative to the outstandingly original human inventions. Besides implying the emergence of something new the word creative is often used, however, with a value-judgement hidden within it. The new is then only called creative if it reveals some form of social or personal worth.[4]

Within evolution itself there is a creative dimension. Genetic types that did not previously exist come into being through natural selection. Rather than any rigid pre-determined uniformity there appears to be a freedom or tolerance for novelty at the heart of evolution : there are no prescribed solutions to the problems of an environment. Men, animals and vegetables survive in waterless deserts or arctic wastes, for example, by a remarkable variety of adaptations to the geo-biological situation.

Indeed, natural selection has been compared to a cybernetic device. Mutations (genetic variations which arise by chance) are 'assessed, accepted or rejected' not in isolation nor solely in the light of information from the environment, but *in relation to the other genes* of the organism in question. Nature matches its colours ! It sees parts always in relation to the whole, and the whole as more than the sum of its parts. Consequently, what is fittest for survival may be a strange combination of strengths and weaknesses, a balance of advantages and disadvantages, abilities and failings.

An internationally known geneticist, Professor Theodosius Dobzhansky, has described this evolutionary process :

> We have, then, not a sieve but a cybernetic device which transfers to the living species 'information' about the state of its environments. This device also makes the evolutionary changes that follow dependent upon those that preceded them. The genetic endowment of a living species contains, therefore, a record of its past environments, as well as an imprint of the present one. This genetic endowment is not a mosaic of genes with autonomous effects; it is an integrated system, the parts of which must fit together to be fit to survive.[5]

In man this natural synthesis, the method of both the 'strategy' of evolution and the 'tactics' of individual growth, has become conscious, in the sense that man knows what he is doing when he makes a tool out of wood and stone whereas a bird fashioning twigs, leaves and mud together into a nest is not aware of what it is doing in the same conscious way.

This does not mean, however, that all of man's synthesizing is done on the conscious level, as when he is making a tool out of wood and metal. If evolution has gradually become aware of itself in man he would expect to find within the less conscious depths of his mind the process of synthesis taking place, namely the putting together of parts of elements so as to make a complex whole. In fact this is what he does find, for it is the witness of many creative people that the welding of apparently disparate or diverse 'parts' into a pattern which is new (in the sense that the resultant whole has not been known before) takes place in the unconscious mind. In many cases evolution is yet more closely matched in that the new 'whole' seems to live and grow with a life of its own, like a baby in the womb. Examples of this unconscious dimension of thinking are given in the following chapter and the reader may care to refer to them now.

Valuing

There is a third theme or mode of thinking which is not finally reducible by or to analysis, or to synthesis or any combination of them, and that is the intellectual activity which I have named *valuing*, or thinking in relation to values or standards. Certainly value-thinking, or valuing should take its place besides analysing and synthesizing as a major form of thinking in its own right. There is a cluster of meanings and associations around this more obscure kind of thinking which to some extent we can separate.

We have seen, for example, that natural selection seems to have its own criteria or standard of values by which it evaluates the kaleidoscopic changes of genetic patterns, namely 'fitness' for survival in the environment. Species may be tested by sudden changes in the environment: those highly adapted to one specific condition may go to the wall, while those with high adaptability will tend to survive.

Man proved able to judge for himself the merit of certain changes as means towards the end of survival. He could appreciate for example the value of fire, or the advantages of metal weapons over stone ones. By extension this kind of valuing or assessing (means in relation to ends) covered all the other end-fulfilling activities of man: the part is judged or evaluated in relation to the whole, and the whole in relation to its purpose. When we judge a horse or dog, for example, we assess it in these inter-related ways. Here the words good or bad simply mean suitable or unsuitable. (Compare the use of the word 'good' in the New Testament phrase 'the good shepherd'. The Greek word for good here, *kalos*, means 'skilled in the craft of' rather than morally good, which would be *agathos*.)

The perception of parts-whole and means-end relations may have led to the more abstract idea of beauty : certainly we find ourselves with that particular idea or 'value', and discussion of its origins can only be speculation. Given the reception of this particular value, however, as part of the information from the cultural environment, it influences the way we see things and the way we make things. The capacity to entertain such abstract constructs is part of our genetic endowment : the actual values we learn or absorb depends largely upon our particular environment.

We may speculate on the evolutionary origins of values, but the fact is that we find them indisputably there in our minds, in varying strengths according to the individual. Moreover, beyond the evolutionary value family already described and their aesthetic town cousins, we find another group living under the same thatched roof : the moral values.

Moral values, the planets that resolve around goodness in the moral sense (the Greek *agathos* as opposed to *kalos*), resemble their town and country relations in that we can discuss them in relation to the *mores* or customs of societies, and how far those invisible rules of standards of behaviour aid or hinder corporate survival. But moral values, without losing their roots in human history, have established a life of their own as interior linings of the mind which may colour the activities both of analysing and synthesizing but do not lend themselves to any dissection. As the philosopher Wittgenstein wrote : 'That which mirrors itself in language, language cannot represent. That which expresses *itself* in language, *we* cannot represent.'[6]

On the other hand it is not to be lightly assumed that moral values have nothing to do with evolution. If evolution is a continuous process and if we can dimly discern the main axis as the advance in the social and individual growth of humanity towards greater diversity combined with a corporate and personal harmony or unity, may it not be that moral values, and particularly the constellation of values around love, are the magnetic forces which bestow an order of meaning or significance to certain external phenomena? In other words, are they not the bearings by which we navigate ourselves towards the undiscovered end of our evolutionary journey? It may be, to change the metaphor, that their radio-activity stems from the fact that they are witnesses to the end of the journey somehow joining us in the middle of it. Values, therefore, may be concerned with a meaning, significance or purpose beyond that anchored so firmly in the instinctive drives of humans, namely the natural activities of surviving, marrying, bearing children and working, whose worth is taken for granted by almost everyone, and questioned only by a few.

The further discussion of the nature of values in the philosophical and theological senses lies outside the scope of this book. The riddle of the universe might well be resolved if we knew who gives value to values, or why values are valued. Here it is sufficient to note the presence of value thinking as being one distinctive mode of thought alongside analysis and synthesis.

Like analysis and creative thinking, the perception and response to values is associated with its own unique range of emotions and feelings. As already suggested, these may serve an evolutionary function, much as pleasure does in connection with eating, by reinforcing our inclination towards the activity.

The capacity for experiencing the range of emotions connected with values obviously varies enormously. Ugliness makes some sick; others care for beauty with a passionate longing. Truth perceived can exhilarate a man and ignorance can depress him. Goodness can delight some men or arouse hatred and scorn in others. We vary in our emotional response to values.

Some of the feelings concerned with values are so relatively mild as to be hardly noticeable : admiration of courage, integrity or selfless love, for example, can have a strangely warming effect upon us. Worship, or worth-ship, the perception of and response to value, which can be closely allied or to compounded of those tender and rare feelings of awe and reverence, is often associated with joy and rejoicing, but more often it is a quieter movement of the whole mind.

Those who experience values and the fine or rare emotions connected with them find them incapable of analysis. In the first place, the act of observation contributes to, influences or changes the situation. Kant spelt this out for philosophers; a child gazing down at a cloud of minnows soon discovers the same truth. It is difficult to see, let alone study, the shy denizens of our own minds.

Professor C. S. Lewis found himself invaded on occasions by joy, but he found it almost impossible to surprise it in return :

You cannot hope and also think about hoping at the same moment; for in hope we look to hope's object and we interrupt this by (so to speak) turning round to look at the hope itself. Of course the two activities can and do alternate with great rapidity; but they are distinct and incompatible. . . . But if so, it followed that all introspection is in one respect misleading. In introspection we try to look 'inside ourselves' and see what is going on. But nearly everything that was going on a moment before is stopped by the very act of our turning to look at it . . . . This discovery flashed a new light back on my whole life. I saw that all my waitings and watchings for Joy, all my vain hopes to find some mental content on which I could, so to speak, lay my finger and say, 'This is it,' had been a futile attempt to contemplate the enjoyed . . . . I should never have to bother again about these images or sensations. I knew that they were merely the mental track left by the passage of Joy – not the wave but the wave's imprint on the sand.[7]

Or, as William Blake wrote :

He who binds to himself a joy
Doth the wingèd life destroy;
But he who kisses the joy as it flies
Lives in eternity's sun-rise.[8]

In the foregoing pages I have tried to separate the single reality of thinking into the three keys of analysis, synthesis and valuing which make up its music. The balance between them is changing from moment to moment : one minute we may be primarily analysing and the next valuing. They have not, however, been so loosened that they are seen as quite separate realities rather than complementary ones. Indeed we may often appreciate this unity more clearly when we contemplate the distortions which occur when one mode of thinking becomes dominant at the expense of the others in a particular individual or group of people.

The Depth Mind Dimension
Thanks to the popularization of the work of Freud and other psycho-analysts it is well-known that our minds include a semi-conscious and an unconscious area. The dichotomizing tendency

in analytical thought has tended to make a sharp distinction between the 'conscious' and 'unconscious' mind. The first is seen often as the seat of reason and order, while the latter is by definition largely unknown, presumed to be peopled by the blind childish impulses and sub-human appetites or desires that we have repressed out of sight and bolted down under trap doors, denizens which come out to play at night in our dreams.

As soon as we start discussing the unconscious mind we naturally resort to images, or vivid graphic mental pictures drawn from everyday life which serve as counters for the indescribable : metaphors or similes pointing us to a reality which they can only partially disclose. Our language for communication with or about the unconscious mind, either internally within ourselves or from person to person, is the language of images, as artists and poets well understand. The closeness of images to the synthesis process is illustrated by the double meaning of imagination as both the 'mental faculty forming images of external objects not present to the senses' and the creative faculty of the mind.

Now the main image used about the mind in this book is borrowed from the work of Marion Miller : the analogy of the sea.[9] Instead of an apparent dichotomy between two compartments of the mind (conscious and unconscious) this image suggests a continuum between surface and depth minds. The picture of the sea allows us to see the light of consciousness penetrating much further from the surface into the 'caverns of the mind' and gradually becoming dimmer in the depths 'no man – fathomed'. In all of the three modes of thinking – analysing, synthesizing and valuing – the depth mind may be involved. Thus we have two inter-related variables : the alternations and interactions of analysing, synthesizing and value-thinking on the one hand and the constant changes and mergings of level between surface and depth minds on the other hand. These variables, taken together with the emotions, begin to give us a model or a general theory of thinking.

The part of the less conscious ranges of the mind in analysis is not often recognized, although, as we shall see later, the depth mind is capable of acting like a computer, unconsciously performing feats of analysis if it is correctly programmed and if certain conditions are present. People vary, however, in the capacity of their depth minds to work in his manner. Intuition, the apprehension of the mind without the intervention of any conscious reasoning process, may describe the instant and immediate eruption into the surface of the mind of some swift piece of depth mind analysis of a total phenomenon. Consequently intuition may be the form of analysis most practised by predominantly holistic minds. (The word holistic comes from the Greek *holas*, meaning whole, and was first coined in 1926 by J. C. Smuts to describe the tendency in nature to produce wholes from the ordered groupings of units. When applied to minds it suggests an intellectual and emotional bias towards seeing life in terms of wholes rather than parts.)

Clearly, if the depth mind can play a part in analysis it follows that a disordered or damaged unconscious dimension in the mind, or a conflict or disconnection between them, can seriously impair or distort the process of analysing. For we do not bring an empty mind to the work of analysis, but one stocked by memory with knowledge, experience and values at various levels of consciousness. Consequently the whole minds of experienced practitioners in a general intellectual situation – e.g. medical, scientific, historical or managerial – may often do their analytical work more speedily, and less consciously than beginners. They may have hunches about a problem which they then proceed to test with their conscious analytical tools.

Writing about the scientist and theologian Teilhard de Chardin, one of his companions on expeditions described the speed with which he invested with significance pre-historic finds in the field : 'In his company, one could always bank on a mental reflex which placed facts in a wider context.... When scrutinizing fossils or artefacts, he gave the impression that he had somehow been involved in their formation, that he could grasp their underlying significance by means of a kind of inner eye. This unusual gift may account for his dislike of expert classification, a necessary task but one which he gladly left to others.'[10]

Even in the mathematical and physical sciences intuitive thinking is essential for work on the frontiers of knowledge. In writing about creativity among mathematicians Hadamard postulated 'scientific taste', which turns out to be often reliable. Some of his subjects, for example, showed flair for choosing profitable lines of work, and for divining intuitively where the work was leading.[11] Writing in 1933 about the nature of scientific discovery Einstein could state : 'There is no logical way to the discovery of these elemental laws. There is only the way of intuition, which is helped by a feeling for the order lying behind the appearance.'[12]

23

Establishing an effective dialogue between surface and depth minds is obviously important if a person's work requires him to make use of the synthetic attributes of his depth mind. For, out of sight of the conscious mind, apparently unrelated facts or ideas may sort themselves out into right relationships with each other, thereby often forming a new unity. This is a natural process of the depth mind, evident also in the paintings and dreams of primitive people and children.

Often this collision and cohesion may be a chance process, without rhyme or reason, like some of the creations in *Alice in Wonderland* in which the author simply allowed two ideas to collide and fuse for the entertainment of children. Other manifestations – in science, art and religion – suggest that the depth mind can grow these constructs like crystals. We shall consider some examples of this unconscious synthesizing in Chapter Two.

Lastly, it remains to note the influence of the levels of consciousness on value-thinking. Although the conscious activity of our surface minds may influence our values in a thousand ways we may properly say that they lie or live in our depth minds 'too deep for words'. They are the *regulae veritatis* or norms of truth, as St Augustine called them, following the Greek philosophers : the norms of truth by which we know truth but which cannot themselves be directly studied or contemplated.[13] The act of turning to study a value cuts us off from the external object which alone brought the latent magnetic feeling into consciousness. Yet we can be aware and catch fleeting glimpses of these values in our depth minds as they colour our thinking, thereby coming to know dimly these roots of our intellectual being.

Thus the depth mind, far from being a zoo without bars, or a chaos of divisive and amoral forces, has the capacity of bringing a natural dimension to the work of sifting information and grasping the relation of parts within a whole presented to it by the senses. It can recapitulate the natural and mysterious life-growth, using ideas and pictorial imagery as the materials from which it fashions living creations. Thus our values are found in our depth minds, or rather in the constant dialogue between surface and depth minds.

Conclusion

To summarize, behind the more-or-less specific activities of problem solving, decision making and creative thinking there lies the more general stream of applied thinking. In its deliberate sense think-ing may be compared to an unfinished symphony with three main themes : analysing, synthesizing and valuing. Behind our conscious thinking in these respects there lie the changing depths of our minds. We cannot, for example, allocate analysis solely to the conscious mind, nor synthesis entirely to the unconscious. Perhaps the first step towards improving our every day thinking is to be-come more aware of the paradoxically simple and yet complex process described so far. Let us now look at and comment upon some examples.

CHAPTER TWO

THINKERS IN ACTION

This chapter contains four case studies of thinkers in different fields. The first two – T. E. Lawrence and General Eisenhower – are given primarily to illustrate decision making. Both are from the military field. This is largely fortuitous. It so happens that soldiers tend to write their autobiographies more often than managers or administrators. Yet there is the advantage that the crises of war tend to bring to the surface factors and influences which are usually more hidden in peacetime situations.

The other two case studies involve scientific discovery and artistic creation. The selection of the people concerned in no way implies that they are more important than anyone else or unique; their decisions or work simply serve as good examples of general principles. As far as creative thinking is concerned I have sought to avoid the better known examples. In the literature some mathematicians and scientists are quoted to the point of becoming almost clichés (Poincaré, Kekulé, Pasteur, etc.), while Sir Lawrence Bragg is virtually unmentioned elsewhere. Nor has C. S. Forester's account of his own creative process as a writer received wide attention.

The sources of the excerpts are given in the Chapter Notes at the back of his book. All the case studies should be read in the light of Chapters One, Three and Eight. Therefore the reader may wish to return to this chapter when he has finished the rest of the book.

T. E. Lawrence
Despite many recent literary attempts to understand the personality of 'Lawrence of Arabia' he still remains something of an enigma. It is clear, however, that in the Arab Revolt of the First World War he played an important part as military adviser to the Arab

26

*leaders. This extract is an account of the intellectual turning-point
in that campaign. Within the larger context of twentieth-century
history it describes a significant moment in the development of
guerrilla fighting as a coherent modern philosophy of warfare. We
join Lawrence and the Arab Army as plans were being made for
them to attack the Turkish forces in Medina early in 1917. While
Lawrence was seeking to co-ordinate the plans he fell ill and for
eight days lay in his tent. As he tossed and turned he began to
think about the campaign as a whole.*

Now, in the field everything had been concrete, particularly
the tiresome problem of Medina; and to distract myself from that
I began to recall suitable maxims on the conduct of modern,
scientific war. But they would not fit, and it worried me. Hitherto,
Medina had been an obsession for us all; but now that I was ill, its
image was not clear, whether it was that we were near to it (one
seldom liked the attainable), or whether it was that my eyes were
misty with too constant staring at the butt. One afternoon I woke
from a hot sleep, running with sweat and pricking with flies, and
wondered what on earth was the good of Medina to us? Its harm-
fulness had been patent when we were at Yenbo and the Turks
in it were going to Mecca : but we had changed all that by our
march to Wejh. Today we were blockading the railway, and they
only defending it. The garrison of Medina, reduced to an in-
offensive size, were sitting in trenches destroying their own power
of movement by eating the transport they could no longer feed.
We had taken away their power to harm us, and yet wanted to
take away their town. It was not a base for us like Wejh, nor a
threat like Wadi Ais. What on earth did we want it for?

The camp was bestirring itself after the torpor of the midday
hours; and noises from the world outside began to filter in to me
past the yellow lining of the tent-canvas, whose every hole and
tear was stabbed through by a long dagger of sunlight. I heard
the stamping and snorting of the horses plagued with flies where
they stood in the shadow of the trees, the complaint of camels,
the ringing of coffee mortars, distant shots. To their burden I
began to drum out the aim in war. The books gave it pat – the
destruction of the armed forces of the enemy by the one process –
battle. Victory could be purchased only by blood. This was a hard
saying for us. As the Arabs had no organized forces, a Turkish
Foch would have no aim? The Arabs would not endure casualties.
How would our Clausewitz buy his victory? Von der Goltz had

seemed to go deeper, saying it was necessary not to annihilate the enemy, but to break his courage. Only we showed no prospect of ever breaking anybody's courage.

However, Goltz was a humbug, and these wise men must be talking metaphors; for we were indubitably winning our war; and as I pondered slowly, it dawned on me that we had won the Hejaz war. Out of every thousand square miles of Hejaz nine hundred and ninety-nine were now free. Did my provoked jape at Vickery, that rebellion was more like peace than like war, hold as much truth as haste? Perhaps in war the absolute did rule, but for peace a majority was good enough. If we held the rest, the Turks were welcome to the tiny fraction of which they stood, till peace or Doomsday showed them the futility of clinging to our window-pane.

I brushed off the same flies once more from my face patiently, content to know that the Hejaz War was won and finished with: won from the day we took Wejh, if we had had wit to see it. Then I broke the thread of my argument again to listen . . .

When it grew too hot for dreamless dozing, I picked up my tangle again, and went on ravelling it out, considering now the whole house of war in its structural aspect, which was strategy, in its arrangements, which were tactics, and in the sentiment of its inhabitants, which was psychology; for my personal duty was command, and the commander, like the master architect, was responsible for all.

The first confusion was the false antithesis between strategy, the aim in war, the synoptic regard seeing each part relative to the whole, and tactics, the means towards a strategic end, the particular steps of its staircase. They seemed only points of view from which to ponder the elements of war, the Algebraical element of things, a Biological element of lives, and the Psychological element of ideas.

The algebraical element looked to me a pure science, subject to mathematical law, inhuman. It dealt with known variables, fixed conditions, space and time, inorganic things like hills and climates and railways, with mankind in type-masses too great for individual variety, with all artificial aids and the extensions given our faculties by mechanical invention. It was essentially formulable.

Here was a pompous, professorial beginning. My wits, hostile to the abstract, took refuge in Arabia again. Translated into Arabic, the algebraic factor would first take practical account of the area we wished to deliver, and I began idly to calculate how many square miles : sixty : eighty : one hundred : perhaps one hundred and forty thousand square miles. And how would the Turks defend all that? No doubt by a trench line across the bottom, if we came like an army with banners; but suppose we were (as we might be) an influence, an idea, a thing intangible, invulnerable, without front or back, drifting about like a gas? Armies were like plants, immobile, firm-rooted, nourished through long stems to the head. We might be a vapour, blowing where we listed. Our kingdoms lay in each man's mind; and as we wanted nothing material to live on, so we might offer nothing material to the killing. It seemed a regular soldier might be helpless without a target, owning only what he sat on, and subjugating only what, by order, he could poke his rifle at.

Then I figured out how many men they would need to sit on all this ground, to save it from our attack-in-depth, sedition putting up her head in every unoccupied one of those hundred thousand square miles. I knew the Turkish Army exactly, and even allowing for their recent extension of faculty by aeroplanes and guns and armoured trains (which made the earth a smaller battlefield) still it seemed they would have need of fortified posts every four square miles, and a post could not be less than twenty men. If so, they would need six hundred thousand men to meet the illwills of all the Arab peoples, combined with the active hostility of a few zealots.

How many zealots could we have? At present we had nearly fifty thousand : sufficient for the day. It seemed the assets in this element of war were ours. If we realized our raw materials and were apt with them, then climate, railway, desert, and technical weapons could also be attached to our interests. The Turks were stupid; the Germans behind them dogmatical. They would believe that rebellion was absolute like war, and deal with it on the analogy of war. Analogy in human things was fudge, anyhow; and war upon rebellion was messy and slow, like eating soup with a knife.

This was enough of the concrete; so I sheered off ἐπιστήμη, the mathematical element, and plunged into the nature of the biological factor in command. Its crisis seemed to be the breaking point, life and death, or less finally, wear and tear. The war-philosophers had properly made an art of it, and had elevated one item, 'effusion of blood', to the height of an essential, which became humanity in battle, an act touching every side of our corporal being, and very warm. A line of variability, Man, persisted like leaven through its estimates, making them irregular. The components were sensitive and illogical, and generals guarded themselves by the device of a reserve, the significant medium of their art. Goltz had said that if you knew the enemy's strength, and he was fully deployed, then you could dispense with a reserve : but this was never. The possibility of accident, of some flaw in materials was always in the general's mind, and the reserve unconsciously held to meet it.

The 'felt' element in troops, not expressible in figures, had to be guessed at by the equivalent of Plato's δόξα, and the greatest commander of men was he whose intuitions most nearly happened. Nine-tenths of tactics were certain enough to be teachable in schools; but the irrational tenth was like the kingfisher flashing across the pool, and in it lay the test of generals. It could be ensued only by instinct (sharpened by thought practising the stroke) until at the crisis it came naturally, a reflex. There had been men whose δόξα so nearly approached perfection that by its road they reached the certainty of ἐπιστήμη. The Greeks might have called such a genius for command νόησις had they bothered to rationalize revolt.

My mind see-sawed back to apply this to ourselves, and at once knew that it was not bounded by mankind, that it applied also to materials. In Turkey things were scarce and precious, men less esteemed than equipment. Our cue was to destroy, not the Turk's army, but his minerals. The death of a Turkish bridge or rail, machine or gun or charge of high explosive, was more profitable to us than the death of a Turk. In the Arab Army at the moment we were chary both of materials and of men. Governments saw men only in mass; but our men, being irregulars, were not formations, but individuals. An individual death, like a pebble dropped in water, might make but a brief hole; yet rings of sorrow widened out therefrom. We could not afford casualties.

Materials were easier to replace. It was our obvious policy to be superior in some one tangible branch; gun-cotton or machine-guns or whatever could be made decisive. Orthodoxy had laid down the maxim, applied to men, of being superior at the critical point and moment of attack. We might be superior in equipment in one dominant moment or respect; and for both things and men we might give the doctrine a twisted negative side, for cheapness' sake, and be weaker than the enemy everywhere except in that one point or matter. The decision of what was critical would always be ours. Most wars were wars of contact, both forces striving into touch to avoid tactical surprise. Ours should be a war of detachment. We were to contain the enemy by the silent threat of a vast unknown desert, not disclosing ourselves till we attacked. The attack might be nominal, directed not against him, but against his stuff; so it would not seek either his strength or his weakness, but his must accessible material. In railway-cutting it would be usually an empty stretch of rail; and the more empty, the greater the tactical success. We might turn our average into a rule (not a law, since war was antinomian) and develop a habit of never engaging the enemy. This would chime with the numerical plea for never affording a target. Many Turks on our front had no chance all the war to fire on us, and we were never on the defensive except by accident and in error.

The corollary of such a rule was perfect 'intelligence', so that we could plan in certainty. The chief agent must be the general's head; and his understanding must be faultless, leaving no room for chance. Morale, if built on knowledge, was broken by ignorance. When we knew all about the enemy we should be comfortable. We must take more pains in the service of news than any regular staff.

I was getting through my subject. The algebraical factor had been translated into terms of Arabia, and fitted like a glove. It promised victory. The biological factor had dictated to us a development of the tactical line most in accord with the genius of our tribesmen. There remained the psychological element to build up into an apt shape. I went to Xenophon and stole, to name it, his word *diathetics*, which had been the art of Cyrus before he struck.

Of this our 'propaganda' was the stained and ignoble offspring. It was the pathic, almost the ethical, in war. Some of it concerned the crowd, an adjustment of its spirit to the point where it became useful to exploit in action, and pre-direction of this changing spirit to a certain end. Some of it concerned the individual, and then it became a rare art of human kindness transcending, by purposed emotion, the gradual logical sequence of the mind. It was more subtle than tactics, and better worth doing, because it dealt with uncontrollables, with subjects incapable of direct command. It considered the capacity for mood of our men, their complexities

31

and mutability, and the cultivation of whatever in them promised to profit our intention. We had to arrange their minds in order of battle just as carefully and as formally as other officers would arrange their bodies. And not only our own men's minds, though naturally they came first. We must also arrange the minds of the enemy, so far as we could reach them; then those other minds of the nation supporting us behind the firing line, since more than half the battle passed there in the back; then the minds of the enemy nation waiting the verdict; and of the neutrals looking on; circle beyond circle.

There were many humiliating material limits, but no moral impossibilities; so that the scope of our diathetical activities was unbounded. On it we should mainly depend for the means of victory on the Arab front : and the novelty of it was our advantage. The printing press, and each newly-discovered method of communication favoured the intellectual above the physical, civilization paying the mind always from the body's funds. We kindergarten soldiers were beginning our art of war in the atmosphere of the twentieth century, receiving our weapons without prejudice. To the regular officer, with the tradition of forty generations of service behind him, the antique arms were the most honoured. As we had seldom to concern ourselves with what our men did, but always with what they thought, the diathetic for us would be more than half the command. In Europe it was set a little aside, and entrusted to men outside the General Staff. In Asia the regular elements were so weak that irregulars could not let the metaphysical weapon rust unused.

Battles in Arabia were a mistake, since we profited in them only by the ammunition the enemy fired off. Napoleon had said it was rare to find generals willing to fight battles; but the curse of this war was that so few would do anything else. Saxe had told us that irrational battles were the refuges of fools : rather they seemed to me impositions on the side which believed itself weaker, hazards made unavoidable either by lack of land room or by the need to defend a material property dearer than the lives of soldiers. We had nothing material to lose, so our best line was to defend nothing and to shoot nothing. Our cards were speed and time, not hitting power. The invention of bully beef had profited us more than the invention of gunpowder, but gave us strategical rather than tactical strength, since in Arabia range was more than force, space greater than the power of armies.

I had now been eight days lying in this remote tent, keeping my ideas general,* till my brain, sick of unsupported thinking, had to be dragged to its work by an effort of will, and went off into a doze whenever that effort was relaxed. The fever passed : my dysentery ceased; and with restored strength the present again became actual to me. Facts concrete and pertinent thrust themselves into my reveries; and my inconstant wit bore aside towards all these roads of escape. So I hurried into line my shadowy principles, to have them once precise before my power to evoke them faded.

It seemed to me proven that our rebellion had an unassailable base, guarded not only from attack, but from the fear of attack. It had a sophisticated alien enemy, disposed as an army of occupation in an area greater than could be dominated effectively from fortified posts. It had a friendly population, of which some two in the hundred were active, and the rest quietly sympathetic to the point of not betraying the movements of the minority. The active rebels had the virtues of secrecy and self-control, and the qualities of speed, endurance and independence of arteries of supply. They had technical equipment enough to paralyse the enemy's communications. A province would be won when we had taught the civilians in it to die for our ideal of freedom. The presence of the enemy was secondary. Final victory seemed certain, if the war lasted long enough for us to work it out.

General Dwight D. Eisenhower
As Supreme Allied Commander Eisenhower had presided over the final planning stages for the largest seaborne military operation of all time: the invasion of Europe in 1944. In the week prior to D-Day Eisenhower's powers as a decision maker came under test.

By the time the operational staffs had moved to Portsmouth, I felt that the only remaining great decision to be faced before D-Day was that of fixing, definitely, the day and hour of the assault. However, the old question of the wisdom of the airborne operation into the Cherbourg peninsula was not yet fully settled in Air Chief Marshal Leigh-Mallory's mind. Later, on May 30 he

---

* Not perhaps as successfully as here. I thought out my problems mainly in terms of Hejaz, illustrated by what I knew of its men and its geography. These would have been too long if written down; and the argument has been compressed into an abstract form in which it smells more of the lamp than of the field. All military writing does, worse luck.

came to me to protest once more against what he termed the 'futile slaughter' of two fine divisions. He believed that the combination of unsuitable landing grounds and anticipated resistance was too great a hazard to overcome. This dangerous combination was not present in the area on the left where the British airborne division would be dropped and casualties there were not expected to be abnormally severe, but he estimated that among the American outfits we would suffer some seventy per cent losses in glider strength and at least fifty per cent in paratroop strength before the airborne troops could land. Consequently the divisions would have no remaining tactical power and the attack would not only result in the sacrifice of many thousand men but would be helpless to affect the outcome of the general assault.

Leigh-Mallory was, of course, earnestly sincere. He was noted for personal courage and was merely giving me, as was his duty, his frank convictions.

It would be difficult to conceive of a more soul-racking problem. If my technical expert was correct, then the planned operation was worse than stubborn folly, because even at the enormous cost predicted we could not gain the principal object of the drop. Moreover, if he was right, it appeared that the attack on Utah Beach was probably hopeless, and this meant that the whole operation suddenly acquired a degree of risk, even foolhardiness, that presaged a gigantic failure, possibly Allied defeat in Europe.

To protect him in case his advice was disregarded, I instructed the air commander to put his recommendations in a letter and informed him he would have my answer within a few hours. I took the problem to no one else. Professional advice and counsel could do no more.

I went to my tent alone and sat down to think. Over and over I reviewed each step, somewhat in the sequence set down here, but more thoroughly and exhaustively. I realized, of course, that if I deliberately disregarded the advice of my technical expert on the subject, and his predictions should prove accurate, then I would carry to my grave the unbearable burden of a conscience justly accusing me of the stupid, blind sacrifice of thousands of the flowers of our youth. Outweighing any personal burden, however, was the possibility that if he were right the effect of the disaster would be far more than local : it would be likely to spread to the entire force.

Nevertheless my review of the matter finally narrowed the critical points to these :

If I should cancel the airborne operation, then I had either to cancel the attack on Utah Beach or I would condemn the assaulting forces there to even greater probability of disaster than was predicted for the airborne divisions.

If I should cancel the Utah attack I would so badly disarrange elaborate plans as to diminish chances for success elsewhere and to maker later maintenances perhaps impossible. Moreover, in long and calm consideration of the whole great scheme we had agreed that the Utah attack was an essential factor in prospects for success. To abandon it really meant to abandon a plan in which I had held implicit confidence for more than two years.

Finally, Leigh-Mallory's estimate was just an estimate, nothing more, and our experience of Sicily and Italy did not, by any means, support his degree of pessimism. Bradley, with Ridgway and other airborne commanders, had always supported me and the staff in the matter, and I was encouraged to persist in the belief that Leigh-Mallory was wrong!

I telephoned him that the attack would go as planned and that I would confirm this at once in writing. When, later, the attack was successful he was the first to call me to voice his delight and to express his regret that he had found it necessary to add to my personal burdens during the final tense days before D-Day . . .

We met with the Meteorologic Committee twice daily, once at 9.30 in the evening and once at 4 in the morning. The committee, comprising both British and American personnel, was headed by a dour but canny Scot, Group Captain J. M. Stagg. At these meetings every bit of evidence was carefully presented, carefully analysed by the experts, and carefully studied by the assembled commanders. With the approach of the critical period the tension continued to mount as prospects for decent weather became worse and worse.

The final conference for determining the feasibility of attacking on the tentatively selected day, June 5, was scheduled for 4 a.m. on June 4. However, some of the attacking contingents had already been ordered to sea, because if the entire force was to land on June 5, then some of the important elements stationed in northern parts of the United Kingdom could not wait for final decision on the morning of June 4.

When the commanders assembled on the morning of June 4 the report we received was discouraging. Low clouds, high winds, and formidable wave action were predicted to make landing a most hazardous affair. The meteorologists said that air support would be impossible, naval gunfire would be inefficient, and even the handling of small boats would be rendered difficult. Admiral Ramsay thought that the mechanics of landing could be handled, but agreed with the estimate of the difficulty in adjusting gunfire. His position was mainly neutral. General Montgomery, properly concerned with the great disadvantages of delay, believed that we should go. Tedder disagreed.

Weighing all factors, I decided that the attack would have to be postponed. This decision necessitated the immediate dispatch of orders to the vessels and troops already at sea and created some doubt as to whether they could be ready twenty-four hours later in case the next day should prove favourable for the assault. Actually the manoeuvre of the ships in the Irish Sea proved most difficult by reason of the storm. That they succeeded in gaining ports, refuelling, and readying themselves to resume the movement a day later represented the utmost in seamanship and in brilliant command and staff work.

The conference on the evening of June 4 presented little, if any, added brightness to the picture of the morning, and tension mounted even higher because the inescapable consequences of postponement were almost too bitter to contemplate.

At 3.30 the next morning our little camp was shaking and shuddering under a wind of almost hurricane proportions and the accompanying rain seemed to be travelling in horizontal streaks. The mile-long trip through muddy roads to the naval headquarters was anything but a cheerful one, since it seemed impossible that in such conditions there was any reason for even discussing the situation.

When the conference started the first report given us by Group Captain Stagg and the meteorologic staff was that the bad conditions predicted the day before for the coast of France were actually prevailing there and that if we had persisted in the attempt to land on June 5 a major disaster would almost surely have resulted. This they probably told us to inspire more confidence in their next astonishing declaration, which was that by the following morning a period of relatively good weather, heretofore completely unexpected, would ensue, lasting probably thirty-six hours. The long-term prediction was not good but they did give us assurance that this short period of good weather would intervene between the exhaustion of the storm we were then experiencing and the beginning of the next spell of really bad weather.

The prospect was not bright because of the possibility that we might land the first several waves successfully and then find later build-up impracticable, and so have to leave the isolated original attacking forces easy prey to German counteraction. However, the consequences of the delay justified great risk and I quickly announced the decision to go ahead with the attack on June 6. The time was then 4.15 a.m., June 5. No one present disagreed and there was a definite brightening of faces as, without a further word, each went off to his respective post of duty to flash out to his command the messages that would set the whole host in motion.

Later a President of the United States, Eisenhower died in 1969. In his memorial speech to Congress, President Nixon cited as a key to Eisenhower's character an undelivered statement prepared in case the Normandy landings during the war ended in disaster. The message read: 'Our landings in the Cherbourg-Havre area have failed to gain a satisfactory foothold and I have withdrawn the troops. My decision to attack at this time and place was based upon the best information available. The troops, the air and navy, did all that bravery and devotion to duty could do. If any blame or fault attaches to the attempt it is mine alone.' Although the message was filed away because the landing was successful: 'That was a man ready to take the consequences of decision,' Mr Nixon concluded. 'That was Eisenhower.'

C. S. Forester

As a novelist C. S. Forester is perhaps best known for his sequence of stories about Horatio Hornblower, a British naval officer in the era of the Napoleonic wars. In this extract from an autobiographical account of his early years the author reflects upon the part played in creation by the unconscious or depth mind:

There are jellyfish that drift about in the ocean. They do nothing to seek out their daily food; chance carries them hither and thither, and chance brings them nourishment. Small living things come into contact with their tentacles, and are seized, devoured and digested. Think of me as the jellyfish, and the captured victims become the plots, the stories, the outlines, the motifs – use whatever term you may consider best to describe the framework of a novel. In the ocean there are much higher forms of life than the jellyfish, and every human being in the ocean of humanity has much the same experience as every other human being, but some human beings are jellyfish and some are sharks. The tiny little food particles, the minute suggestive experiences, are recognized and seized by the jellyfish writer and are employed by him for his own specialized use.

We can go on with the analogy; once the captured victim is inside the jellyfish's stomach the digestive juices start pouring out and the material is transformed into a different protoplasm, without the jellyfish consciously doing anything about it until his existence ends with an abrupt change of analogy.

In my own case it happens that, generally speaking, the initial stimulus is recognized for what it is. The casual phrase dropped by a friend in conversation, the paragraph in a book, the incident observed by the roadside, has some special quality, and is accorded a special welcome. But, having been welcomed, it is forgotten or at least ignored. It sinks into the horrid depths of my subconscious like a waterlogged timber into the slime at the bottom of a harbour, where it lies alongside others which have preceded it. Then, periodically – but by no means systematically – it is hauled up for examination along with its fellows, and, sooner or later, some timber is found with barnacles growing on it. Some morning when I am shaving, some evening when I am wondering whether my dinner calls for white wine or red, the original immature idea reappears in my mind, and it has grown. Nearly always it has something to do with what eventually will be the mid-point of a novel or a short story, and sometimes the growth is towards the end and sometimes towards the beginning. The casualty rate is high – some timbers grow no barnacles at all – but enough of them have progressed to keep me actively employed for more than forty years.

Examination completed, the timber is dropped back again into the slime, to be fished out every now and then until the barnacles are found to be quite numerous. That is when the plot is really beginning to take shape; that is when the ideas relating to it recur to me more and more often, so that they demand a greater and greater proportion of my attention as the days go by, until, in the end, the story might almost be described as an obsession, colouring my thoughts and influencing my actions and my behaviour. Generally some real work is called for at this stage, to clear up some mechanical difficulty. At some point in the plot it may be essential for the *Lydia* and the *Natividad* to be at the same place at the same time – what forces (other than pure coincidence) can bring this about? What has happened earlier that makes it quite inevitable? A different kind of inventiveness has to be employed here.

This sort of difficulty is sometimes cleared up in a peculiar and often gratifying fashion – I have known it to happen half a dozen times. I have been developing two different plots, both of them vaguely unsatisfactory, and then suddenly they have dovetailed together, like two separate halves of a jigsaw puzzle – the difficulties have vanished, the story is complete, and I am experiencing a special, intense pleasure, a glow of satisfaction – entirely undeserved – which is perhaps the greatest reward known to my profession . . .

It was odd how that story haunted me. Then it began, the old familiar stirring of the emotions, the feeling of recognition, the knowledge that something was about to take shape. And so it did – with everything coming at once. That had happened before, and would happen again. I do not understand why it is, that when I am constructing a story which is quite episodic, the episodes should all take form at once, or as nearly as my capacity allows. One day all the episodes are chaotic, formless, and then on a later day, not so long afterwards, they have all taken shape and are arranging themselves in order – I had had the same experience with the *Midshipman* as well as with other books.

There have been occasions when psychologists have questioned me to discover the mechanisms of these processes. They call them 'creative', but that is a misnomer; the eventual result is creation, if such a self-satisfied word can be tolerated, but the processes are to a large extent – are almost entirely – involuntary. Does a chicken lay an egg because she wants to or because she has to? Just possibly the writer may assist, or speed up, his processes by making himself receptive, by offering hospitality to the wandering idea, but I not only do not believe it but I am inclined to think the opposite is true. Certainly there is a danger point at which there is a sharp transition between being receptive and trying to force the process; if ideas are forced the result is nearly always – let us say invariably – hackneyed or unnatural or pedantic. The average Hollywood story conference is a deliberate attempt to force the formation of ideas.

So far in my life I have flinched from going more deeply into this question; when the psychologists have started to probe I have always remembered how easy it is to take a watch to pieces and how hard it is to make it go again. Maybe my ideas come because, deeply rooted, there is something wrong with me, which analysis might cure. If this is so I cannot think of a better example of the remedy being worse than the disease. I have no desire whatever to be cured of something which has piled interest into my life from boyhood until now, and I hardly expect to grow so old that I shall decide that there is sufficiently little in the future to lose, and submit to analysis to discover the cause of the flow.

Sir Lawrence Bragg

Sir Lawrence Bragg is one of the foremost scientists in the world. He is the only one who has ever lived to celebrate the fiftieth anniversary of winning his Nobel Prize. His work was X-ray crystallography – the interpretation of peculiar patterns obtained by shining beams of X-rays through a crystal. In 1912 Bragg suddenly realized that they contained the vital clue to the way atoms were arranged in different substances. The most famous of these substances – the DNA molecule – is the blueprint of heredity. Its structure was solved in 1953 by Francis Crick and James Watson while working under Bragg. On this account many scientists have put Bragg's discovery on a level of importance with that of nuclear fission. What kind of mind did he possess? In order to illustrate some the general statements about creative and inventive people in Chapter Six here are some excerpts from a programme about Sir Lawrence Bragg televised by the BBC in 1965.

FRANCIS CRICK : I think the great quality that attracts one about Bragg is his enthusiasm, almost his boyish enthusiasm. There was a time when I was being rather critical about the work going on in the lab. and he said to me : 'Crick, you're rocking the boat.' By which he meant, you're destroying the confidence of the people who were working. And it was because of this enthusiasm that he attracted exceptionally good people to work for him. He made research exciting and I think basically it was because he enjoyed the aesthetic appeal of good science – it was simple and it was beautiful.

COMMENTARY : As well as being one of the most distinguished living scientists, Bragg is an extremely capable artist, a brilliant lecturer – especially to children – and a highly talented and popular grandfather. And he is perhaps unique among great scientists for the warmth and affection he inspires in his colleagues and even his rivals. Although he is seventy-five, Bragg is still very much on top of his subject. He founded X-ray crystallography fifty years ago, and he has led it and presided over it ever since – he's seen it grow from a single idea into a subject studied all over the world.

BARRY WESTWOOD : Sir Lawrence, you were as I know, born and brought up in Australia because your father had gone out there to be Professor of Physics and Mathematics at Adelaide University. How far were you influenced towards being a scientist by the fact that your father was one?

BRAGG : A great deal. I think that's bound to happen in a family. It was not only my father's interests, things he used to tell me about when I was quite young, six or seven (my favourite bedtime story was my father telling me all about atoms, hydrogen, oxygen and so on), but as well as that there's the general atmosphere, the fact that he had a laboratory, the fact that he had a head of the laboratory who used to make scientific toys for us to play with, little electrical things that worked and so on. All that influences a boy's hobbies very much. And then of course my grandfather was a scientist too. My mother's father – he was Postmaster General and Astronomer Royal of South Australia, two posts which I always thought inevitably went together. But that meant that he had all the Government stores out of the Observatory. I'm afraid my brother Bob and I used to raid those and beg all sorts of bits of wire and so on and make things with it, and so I naturally began to take a great interest in anything that worked scientifically.

WESTWOOD : You were really something of an infant prodigy, weren't you? You went to Adelaide University I think at the extraordinarily early age of fifteen, took a First Class Honours degree in maths at the age of eighteen and also by that young age made an original contribution towards scientific knowledge. Remember this?

BRAGG : Oh! I should think so! Yes indeed. Of course I was very unevenly developed. I think perhaps I was rather forward with the intellectual side but very backward indeed on the games and that kind of thing, and so I rather took to somewhat lonely hobbies

41

and one of the great ones was shell collecting. I had quite a good collection of South Australian shells, but this really I am proud of because it was given my name and still bears it. Nobody's challenged the species. It's a little bone of a cuttlefish, very dainty little cuttlefish called Sepia Braggi. It was named by Dr Virco who was the great authority in Australia and I remember very well indeed, I took it to him and he verified it was new; he said, I think I shall call it 'Sepia Gondola' because it looks so like a Venetian gondola, and then, I must have been about twelve or thirteen at the time – I think he saw my face fall and he said, 'No, we'll call it Sepia Braggi.' And there it is . . .

WESTWOOD : Then in 1912 this historic picture was published by the German scientist von Laue, and it was really the correct interpretation of the spots on this picture which led you on to your Nobel Prize work. I believe that it was whilst you were walking along the Backs in St John's College in Cambridge that you had this idea of the correct solution. Can you remember how you felt?

BRAGG : Very vividly indeed. I remember it almost as if it were yesterday, I'd been thinking a great deal about this picture of von Laue's – studying it and wondering what it meant – and as always in science, it was the putting of several things together that led to the answer. C. T. R. Wilson's brilliant lectures on optics and the relation of pulses to spectral light, J. J. Thomson on X-rays, and talk about crystals (we had a little society) and I suppose one's unconscious mind works on these things – but I do remember so vividly walking along the Backs and suddenly seeing that there was a much simpler way of looking at phenomenon than the rather complex one which Laue had developed. And that was it, that's what started me . . .

PROFESSOR DOROTHY HODKIN : Sir Lawrence Bragg was already a legend when I first began X-ray analysis in the early 1930s. I remember Bernal telling us that when he was working with Sir Lawrence's father at the Royal Institution, they always sent any structures that proved too difficult for them to tackle to Manchester to be solved by Sir Lawrence Bragg. It was at Manchester that I first saw him when I casually visited the laboratory there, never expecting to see him. I was most proud and delighted that he spoke to me and tremendously impressed by his great kindness and his interest in one so young and unknown. Later I remember again at a meeting in Manchester that he was discussing the problem of the structure of proteins, and added 'the solution of which we shall all live to see'. I had a sense of immediate concern – did he really realize how very difficult this problem was? And this concern was followed by a wave of hopefulness that he might prove to be correct, as indeed he has done.

WESTWOOD : Sir Lawrence, do you remember that remark about proteins – 'The solution we shall live to see' – made thirty or more years ago.

BRAGG : I remember my enthusiasm and my hope at the time – I don't know that I remember the exact remark. People seem to remember a number of wonderful remarks I made which I've quite forgotten.

WESTWOOD : You say you had hope at the time – was it hope, or were you confident even that far back that this would ultimately be done?

BRAGG : Well, you know, it's a strange thing but I do feel in science that if you're absolutely determined to get a thing out you generally get it out. It's wonderful in that way how often that does happen. Science is very much a matter of sticking to it.

WESTWOOD : You've always got on remarkably well with children, haven't you?

BRAGG : Yes . . .

WESTWOOD : And it seems . . .

BRAGG : And I think I can say that, partly because I'm rather a case of arrested development and find it easy to understand them.

WESTWOOD : It seems also that they find it easy to understand and like you, at least according to your wife that's so.

LADY BRAGG : My husband has a magnetic attraction for children. Part of his mind, I think, is still a child's mind. I remember once

43

when we were crossing the Atlantic a small boy attached himself to him. His mother was seasick and he was all alone. He came up to my husband and said, 'Could you show me a whale?' My husband said, 'Well it's very rare to see a whale at this time of year, but come along, we'll walk round the ship.' They walked round the ship and there was no whale. But suddenly, just at the end, my husband said 'Look!' and there was a whale really doing its stuff and spouting. The little boy just looked at my husband and said, 'Can I stay with you always.'

FRANCIS CRICK : When Jim Watson and I were working on the structure of DNA we were doing it by building models in Bragg's lab. And I think it's an interesting question to ask : What did we learn from Bragg that helped us to solve that structure? Well, of course, through being in the Cavendish we had a lot of technical know-how – how you actually went about building models, all about lengths and angles and distances and the details of crystallography and helical differentials and in some ways, one of them was a little unexpected. That was, we learned not to put too much trust in the experimental evidence. Now when you're a student you're always taught you must of course observe the facts and that's what science is about. When you come to do research you find that this can be very misleading. Sometimes the facts aren't right – sometimes they just put you off the scent, even though they're correct, as they did in the case of the alpha helix which Bragg didn't solve and Pauling did, partly because of one experimental fact to which they paid too much attention. The other thing we learned, I think, was something a little more intangible, it was the style of attack, the way of looking at a problem, not getting involved in the detail too much, making a simple hypothesis, working it out, seeing how it fitted the broad run of the evidence and if it led to something interesting and unexpected. People are taught this but you actually learn it by seeing somebody do it. Of course, the real skill comes in telling actually *when* a problem is simple. And I suppose we must have learned a bit of that too, because Bragg has this particular power and that's why he's often been so successful in his work.

WESTWOOD : Now the solution of the structure of DNA is undoubtedly one of the great scientific highlights of the century and many people would say, the equivalent to splitting the atom.

BRAGG : I think eventually it will prove to be so.

WESTWOOD : And then it went on, this work on protein structures, to solve some incredibly complex structures, notably the work of Perutz and Kendrew who themselves in the same year, 1962, got the Nobel Prize for Chemistry.

BRAGG : Yes.

MAX PERUTZ : I have always been tremendously impressed by the speed and clarity of Bragg's mind and by his power of scientific judgment. While others doubt and hesitate, Bragg will see the importance of a scientific discovery in a flash. If he conceives a scientific idea of his own he goes home in the evening to write it up and comes back next morning with the finished paper ready for the typist – rather like Mozart writing the Overture to 'The Marriage of Figaro' in a single night. Not a word needs changing. His mind leaps like a prima ballerina, with perfect ease. What is so unique about it – and this is what made his lectures so marvellous – is the combination of penetrating logic and visual imagery. Many of his successes in crystal structure analysis are due to this power of visualizing the aesthetically and physically most satisfying way of arranging a complicated set of atoms in space and then having found it, with a triumphant smile, he would prove the beauty and essential simplicity of the final solution.

WESTWOOD : And in a sense it's true isn't it that all the things which we've mentioned, sound ranging, radio astronomy, crystallography, all are concerned with spatial relationships?

BRAGG : Yes. Of course that's so. My wife always puts that rather clearly I think– she always asks why we're making models. It's one of the few, perhaps the only advantage of science, where the essence of what you discover is a model. A number of things in the right – the relative – positions to each other.

WESTWOOD : One of your friends raises this point quite clearly.

SIR GEORGE THOMSON : I sometimes wondered what would have happened if Willie had ever run out of crystals. Was it luck? After all, he came into crystallography at the ideal time for it and him and he had the ideal equipment. Now just suppose there hadn't been any more crystals – would he have been a great scientist for the rest of his life? I am sure he would. He is not a one-idea man.

WESTWOOD : Do you think of yourself as a one-idea man?

BRAGG : I often think of myself as a no-idea man. When I think back in the history of all this work, to try and trace where the beginning of where any of it came from, I always remember some student, some friend who tipped me off with a remark of some kind that set me thinking.

WESTWOOD : Now this positive spate of Nobel Prizes in 1962, all arising basically out of the work for which you yourself had got the Nobel Prize nearly fifty years earlier, must have been very exciting for you. In fact your wife remembers quite clearly when the news came through.

LADY BRAGG : He was pretty ill at the time. I rushed round to the hospital with the news. He was terribly thrilled. He spent the night explaining protein structures in detail to the little Irish night nurse who listened very patiently but didn't understand a word. Next day the doctor said to me : 'Well he's over the worst, but now I think he may die of excitement . . .'

WESTWOOD : You really love lecturing, don't you?

BRAGG : Yes, I do. I really enjoy it, and I think there really is a great artistic pleasure in making an experiment not only work, but work so that it looks aesthetically attractive, and with the maximum of simplicity.

WESTWOOD : Well, I know that this imagination that you have leads you not only to the study of crystal structures, but also to express yourself very well indeed, in paint and pencil and crayon, but you draw and paint a great deal. I know, for instance, that you've sketched most of your family; and now as a grandfather you combine, obviously with great joy, the artistic gift which you have with the love which you have for children . . .

46

WESTWOOD : Sir Lawrence, your wife just said that you're really a very private character, so let me ask you only with reference to your scientific life, what have been the highlights?

BRAGG : They have, as I suppose with all scientists, been the times when one has suddenly seen the answer. It always comes – it's a curious feeling, it's a revelation rather that one's discovered something oneself as if one had been told the answer. I remember it in the very early work with the Laue photograph; I remember it in our work on silicates; I remember it, perhaps very vividly indeed, in the protein. Of course, it was Perutz who made the great tactical advance that made it possible – we ran into difficulties with his crystal – Kendrew it was who got out the first one, he sent me some of his results, and I played with them, he was doing the real work, but, I just saw for the first time, suddenly, the answer is there! It's going to go! I think that was perhaps the greatest moment of a scientific discovery in my life.

And then I suppose what gave me the deepest pleasure was when I heard about the four Nobel Prizes. I'm sure that ranked much higher than my hearing about my own in World War One. But as I look back, I can't help thinking the whole time of the young researchers. It's hard to think of any one of the great discoveries in which I don't have the feeling – well that, really, that idea was put to me by so-and-so or so-and-so and perhaps to sum it up, that very few of them indeed can I say stemmed from me – they rather happened where I was.

In order to complete the picture it is relevant to quote Sir Lawrence Bragg's views on the relation of science to moral values, for they further illustrate the qualitative differences between analysis, synthesis and value thinking. In a reply printed in The Times *to a newspaper article by Dr Edmund Leach, Provost of King's College, Cambridge, which made large claims for the role of science in life, Sir Lawrence had this to say:*

May I comment as a scientist on Dr Leach's article (November 16, 1968) on the responsibilities of scientists? The word 'science' is often loosely used to cover two quite different forms of human endeavour.

There is on the one hand the search for a deeper understanding of Nature. In this search one cannot distinguish between knowledge which could be put to good uses and that which could be turned to bad ends. The distinction is meaningless, and in any case it is hardly ever possible to guess to what use a new and fundamental advance can be put, at the time it is made; the future holds so many surprises.

This knowledge goes into a store from which industry draws the many items of information it wants in order to achieve its technical ends. The word 'science' is used in this latter case to stand for the technical achievements which are made possible by this deeper knowledge, and the vastly greater powers over Nature which they provide. Science has greatly amplified the powers of invention which man always employed to effect his purposes. Scientists have a deep responsibility not only for suggesting 'how it can be done' but also for foreseeing as best they can the possible dangers of exploiting these powers rashly. But the decision as to the ends to be achieved involves moral questions on which science as such has no authority to dictate, as others of your correspondents have stressed, and I am sure that responsible scientists would not wish to claim any such authority.

Not so long ago, science could point with some complacency to the advantage it had brought in comfort and health, ease of travel and communication, and opportunities to share in culture. Now it is not on so good a wicket. The advances in technology have been so embarrassingly rapid, and have raised so many new and difficult problems, that it is natural to wonder if the losses outweigh the gains from the Pandora's Box which we have opened.

But is not this taking too short a view? The portents show that we are entering on one of those times when the way of life profoundly changes. The last great change was the introduction of agriculture which made it possible for men to live in communities and so changed savagery into civilization. Civilization was based on a greater control of Nature. We can only dimly guess about this new 'X', based on technical achievements which bind the whole world so closely, but cannot it be foreseen that 'X' will be some higher form of social integration which bears the same relation to civilization as the latter did to savagery?

This is the challenge we are facing and man must try to guide his course by the 'Wisdom whose price is above rubies' which exists in a dimension for which science has no measuring scale.

CHAPTER THREE

DECISION MAKING

In the first chapter we looked at the intellectual themes which the mind weaves into the music of thought. In the last pages we have seen some examples of thinking drawn from a range of human experience and selected to illustrate the part played by the depth mind. Many managers or supervisors reading the book may have wondered in what ways the experience of generals, writers and scientists can be relevant to their own decision making and problem solving. The object of this chapter is to show how the universal mental abilities of analysing, synthesizing and valuing combine or interlock together in ever-changing kaleidoscopic patterns when we set about making a decision, and that the depth mind is necessarily involved at all stages, not just during the phase often labelled 'incubation' by many writers on creative thinking. Understanding this process should help us later on to improve our performance, both in learning to make better decisions ourselves and also in helping others to do the same.

What is a decision?

First, let us be clear upon what we mean by a 'decision'. By one extreme definition almost everything we do involves making decisions; by another, at the other end of the scale, we make only a few real decisions in our lives. The first school of opinion would hold that a manager spends almost all his time decision making; the second school declares that he makes few real decisions, but that they are highly significant events.

The *Shorter Oxford English Dictionary* gives us three current meanings for the word: (1) the action of deciding (a contest, question etc.); settlement, determination; a conclusion, judgement; especially one formally pronounced in a court of law:

(2) the making up of one's mind; a resolution; (3) as a quality: determination, firmness, decidedness of character. The word itself comes from Latin and means 'to cut off'. By giving the victory to one side or the other, you 'cut off' the mental process of weighing both sides – or all angles – of a question, controversy or cause.

Note that the word implies some form of preliminary confusion or hesitation. Where there is no choice involved we do not have the experience of making a decision, or (because 'to do nothing' is usually a viable alternative in most situations) we experience it only in a mild form. If you want to get work and you are offered only one job, there is hardly a decision to be made. But if there are two equally inviting offers then you are in the decision-making situation.

Leadership decisions

The broad definition given above excludes the large areas which are 'programmed' by the computer of our depth minds, for example, the now almost unconscious repetitions of previous decisions we call 'habits'. On the other hand, the range of situations in which we make decisions in the defined sense is as wide as life itself. Nor can our decisions be kept in tidy compartments in our lives: we may have to choose the curtains in the office as well as at home, and ethical choice can pose themselves for decision by any way-side.

Yet there are decisions which we may describe as distinctly managerial, or, to widen the field to include all groups, organizations and societies, decisions which are the characteristic responsibility of leaders. These are decisions which involve selecting the best means of achieving the common goal.

On the whole people associate together in groups or organizations because there is a task to be done which one person cannot do on his own. Leadership is needed if the common task is to be achieved, not only to maintain the unity or cohesiveness of the group but to ensure that the necessary choices or decisions are made which will lead to the attainment of the objective. As we can say that management is the form that leadership assumes in the industrial or commercial environment, it follows that managerial decisions are those which concern selecting and implementing that course of action in a given situation which will lead to maximum results in terms of the aims of the company.

At the highest level of industry these can – and indeed will – almost invariably involve major policy decisions. The Chairman of Unilever, Dr Ernest Woodroofe, recently gave an example of such a decision, which could of course be matched by the chairmen or directors of any other company :

> A couple of years ago, one section of our business proposed that we should expand into yoghurt and dairy products. There was a natural link up with our existing cheese business and it was brand marketing of the kind in which we have some expertise. Much was in our favour. We knew a lot about the scientific and technological aspects of milk in our ice-cream and margarine businesses, about the distribution of chilled and frozen products. Our crystal ball seemed to indicate that more and more food products would be sold from the chilled cabinets in the shops. However, there were some very strongly entrenched competitors with well-known brand names and, of course, some of the super-markets sell under their own names. We weighed the pros and cons and decided to back the proposal. We are well satisfied with our decision because, although we have had to withdraw in this country, we are making good progress on the continent of Europe.[1]

Five steps in decision making

Among writers on decision making there is broad agreement on the main phases or steps of the process. It should be emphasized, however, that the following summary of those steps is not designed to be a rigid and inflexible framework. One can have trained and disciplined thought without a fastidious concern for mental tidiness. Indeed, the 'scientific method' often held up as an example for the manager is not capable of being codified into a mental drill or procedure, except by hindsight.

Thus the five stages or steps outlined below might be compared to musical notes which can be arranged by the mind in any order. In analysing and presenting them it is convenient to use a logical sequence, but the reader should remember that this pattern is really a temporary and artificial one. For a variety of good reasons, one step may be missed out altogether. The five can be arranged like dance steps into any number of sequences – minuets, waltzes, sambas – according to individual idiosyncrasy and the prevailing circumstances. The music which both accompanies and invades the steps is made up of the three main themes of analysis, synthesis and valuing. We cannot arrange the latter into sequence and allocate them separately to one or more of the steps. In each of the overlapping and ever-changing set of five phases the three major forms of deliberate thinking may well be present in differing proportions.

Similarly, we cannot exclude the depth mind from each of the phases. This is particularily true when the time-span for a decision encompasses more than a few minutes or hours. But it leads us on to the central point that the mind can do a lot of work in the five areas when it is 'off-line' (to use a computer term). Indeed, there may be a close relation between this kind of background preparatory (but nevertheless directed) thinking and the ease with which a person makes decisions when he finds himself in a situation which demands a choice. Paradoxically, many decisions are decided before we make them : we come into situations with our minds made up in the sense that some possible courses are ruled out and certain values deeply seated in our minds. The relation of decisions to thinking is rather like that of battles to war : battles are only high peaks in a mountain range of military activity in which such 'depth' realities as economics and morale are much more important in the long run than any single encounter, won or lost.

With these considerations in mind the five steps or phases of decision making will be discussed in turn.

SPECIFY THE AIM
Almost all books and articles on decision making highlight the cardinal importance of being sure that you know what you want to do. The first principle of war is 'select and maintain your aim', and all military 'appreciations' (or written decision-making exercises) begin with a consideration of the aim. Similarly the literature on management and organizational leadership generally stresses the need to determine or specify what is one's task.

For the sake of clarity useful distinctions can be drawn between purpose, aims and objectives both for organizations and individuals. The *purpose* is the ultimate end that the organization is there to serve. Inevitably this will be stated in very general or abstract language, if it is put into words at all. By asking the question 'why?' for long enough we can reach the realm of purpose – the overall direction of an enterprise or a society – but our minds are not made to linger for long in a landscape of unrelieved abstract words. We may catch glimpses or insights, however, that in these higher reaches of purpose there is ultimately a fusion of action (or purposeful living) with values. The ability to think at the level of purpose or make decisions in the terms of values is certainly a characteristic displayed by leaders, especially those at a senior level.

In order to make decisions at this level the manager needs both a sense of responsibility and a set of values to which he adheres with integrity. Dr Ernest Woodroofe, from the viewpoint of being chairman of a company which employs 320,000 people in seventy countries and is the tenth largest company in the world, offered this definition of integrity :

> Most decisions in business are based on uncertainties because you don't have all the information you would theoretically like to have, but having what you have, you must use your judgement and decide. But, and this is what I mean by the overriding importance of integrity, the decision must be made within the framework of the responsibilities the business man carries. He has responsibilities to the shareholders, the employees, the consumer, even the Government of the day. He has to balance these responsibilities thoroughly, justly and without bias. You could, for instance, make a decision which was to the benefit of your shareholders, but to the detriment of the community as a whole. *Not* doing that, and knowing why you are not going to do it, and what not doing it is going to cost you, is what I mean by integrity.[2]

The exploration of the purpose of industry and commerce as a whole (from which individual companies and firms derive their purpose) leads one to see it in the wider concentric contexts of the given society and political situation, humanity and natural resources and the fulfilment of individual needs, both material and personal. The really hard managerial decisions at the top level are those which involve apparent or real conflicts between these responsibilities which taken together combine to constitute the single purpose of industry and commerce. The capacity to see clearly at the level of purpose, which implies seeing long-term consequences of decisions, is perhaps what is meant by vision.

We tend to speak of purpose in the singular : it has an integrating unity about it, like a broad river flowing towards an undiscovered sea. The tributaries which feed the river (and are fed by it) we might call the *aims* of an organization. They are more specific and defined than purpose. Statements of aims begin with infinitive such has 'to manufacture such-and-such goods'. Obviously an organization can and almost certainly must have several aims which hinge together in a common purpose.

Lastly, we come to *objectives*, which are aims broken down into specific goals or targets, two concrete metaphors from the football field and the archery butts which imply an objective clearly seen within a limited time-and-space context. An objective or aim is often given to the decision maker, and all that he has to do is state it and check it. But the higher he climbs in any organization the less he can take for granted the apparently 'given' objective or aim and the more the first step in decision making assumes importance. It is sometimes said that a problem stated is a problem half-solved. It is equally true that an aim correctly stated is a decision half-made. When they are not in the situation of having a decision to make leaders often ask themselves : 'What business are we in? What are we trying to do or achieve in the next five years?'

Consequently the purpose, aims and objectives which are implicit in an organization (or explicit in the decision maker's brief) must be subjected to analysis. This means that their complexities should be unravelled and explored, so that the relation between them becomes apparent. Analysis, however short, should serve to confirm or replace the given objective or aim.

Synthetic thinking comes into play in the mental creation of aims and objectives. The ability to 'put together' the abstract and ideal with the concrete and the practical is necessary for the construction or definition of the kind of aims or objectives to which people will respond in the industry of the future. Even objectives do not just happen : someone has to put together or combine certain elements, just as an archery target is made up of straw, wood, paint, cord and canvas, sewn into an identifiable whole.

The ability to see ideas, people and things as parts of an integrated whole clearly serves the middle or senior manager well, and it should complement his analytical powers. Often he may be a holistic thinker as well in the sense that consciously or unconsciously he sees the purpose of the organization as growth. The tendency of nature to produce a whole from the ordered groupings of units seems also to work in organizations, often heedless of other factors, as Parkinson's Law humorously proclaims. Growth can (consciously or unconsciously) become a criterion of success, as the ardent 'empire-builder' has recognized. The manager sees himself more as a farmer or gardener : feeding and watering here, cutting and pruning there, and justly enjoying the fruits of his labours. Growth, despite all the problems it brings, is seen to be

54

closer to the purpose than profit making, yet it is a growth which the managerial gardener must carefully regulate so that the organization expands neither too quickly or too slowly.

Whether or not size is an end in itself and a value to be pursued is a question which requires much more attention. Perhaps we have uncritically accepted a hidden value-judgement in the exciting (to holistic minds) idea of 'growth'. Sometimes a decrease in size might also be a measure of success.

Yet in the step of decision making which clusters round consideration of the aim, the intellectual activities of analysing and synthesizing are not alone. Perhaps at no other point does that deliberate thinking we have called here valuing so much need to come into play. In the case of a given objective or aim there should be some sort of scanning device which checks it against deeply held values. What used to be called a bad conscience (in reality a good conscience doing its work) may be compared to a radar screen that illuminates some identified or unrecognized object. An objective is not held to be morally or legally defensible because someone told you to attain it, as a generation of Nazi leaders discovered.

The conscience, however, is an emergency signal. Value thinking is best done out of the decision-making situation; in the quiet and calmness of the depth mind our values take shapes only partly known to us. Purpose, if not aims, implies values, for they are the directional compass bearings by which we guide ourselves in the choices of our lives. Like a sports player, the effective decision maker has done much of his work off the field : often the race is won or lost before it has begun. Similarly, those with a clear and useable frame of reference, or hierarchy of values, will avoid perhaps the worst fate of any decision maker – not knowing what he really wants to do.

REVIEWING THE FACTORS

The hardest part of decision making is being certain about your objective or aim in the teeth of possible contenders for its position. The next lot of untidy or irregular bursts of analysing, synthesizing and valuing cluster round the factors, the major elements or synthetic constructs of the facts which shape or shadow the situation. Facts come to us ready made in constellations that we call factors : they may have to be unpacked and re-assembled. We may of course be aware of the factors long before we define the aim or objective, but once we sense that a decision has to be made it is a good idea to take a fresh look at the factors and to see them in relation to the decision.

Factor analysis has received much attention, and we can summarize the advice which the text-books offer us :

(i) List and name (or identify) all the major factors which are self-evidently important, and those minor ones which could have some influence on the achievement of the aim. For example, a general may have to consider : relative strengths, ground, time and space, climatic conditions, security and courses open to enemy.

(ii) Continually ask yourself when weighing a factor : 'So what?' If the answer does not add up to much then the factor is not worth considering. The answer to the question 'So what?' is the deduction. Vague and indecisive deductions are not of much use : deductions must be clear, definite and relevant. In other words, each factor must be 'squeezed dry' until it has yielded all it has to give.

(iii) Search for the critical factor, the one upon which the making of the decision really hinges. It is not always there, but seeking for it is a valuable way of turning over the ground.

(iv) Look at all the factors taken together. Here synthetic thinking comes into play to balance undue concentration on one factor or set of factors. The combined influence of all the factors, the mysterious sum of the situation which is more than all its parts, needs to be sensed or felt. Whereas the analyst may be competent at dissecting the factors in a situation, his judgement will be impaired if he lacks a sense of the whole picture.

Again, both value-thinking and the depth mind can be heavily involved in the consideration of factors. Obviously our own values and the values of other individuals, the organization, or society, can be factors in their own right, and may well turn out to be the critical factor. The depth mind, providing we do not disturb its work with worry or anxiety, is adept at the holistic work of seeing factors as a whole.

COURSES OPEN

Having examined and turned over all the relevant factors it should become clear that there are a number of courses of action or possible decisions open to us. There again have to be listed, either mentally or on paper.

Through lack of imagination or circumspection we may easily

miss possible courses of action. Our minds have a tendency to dichotomize, i.e. to see reality in terms of either/or, and we carry this bias with us into the decision-making situation. In particular it manifests itself in the mirage of there being only two mutually-exclusive courses open to us, whereas in fact there may be many more if we think hard. This tendency is reflected in the way that the word 'alternative' (which means literally one or other of two things, the choice of one implying the rejection of the other) has come to be used instead of 'possibility' (of which there can be many). We see life in terms of alternatives rather than possibilities, and are not aware that we are doing so.

Visualizing or recognizing a dichotomy because one is wearing mental blinkers must not be confused with the scanning process whereby many courses of action or possible decisions are steadily reduced to a short list of two runners. The either/or approach, especially when it becomes a mental habit, is dangerous because it over-simplifies reality. This may have been the fundamental flaw in the decision making of Adolf Hitler (after his abysmal set of values). Albert Speer, one of the Fuehrer's intimates, noted this trait. 'His close associates even openly made fun of Hitler, without his taking offence.' Thus his standard phrase, 'There are two possibilities,' would be used by one of his secretaries, in his presence, often in the most banal of contexts. She would say : 'There are two possibilities. Either it is going to rain or it is not going to rain.'[3]

Experienced decision makers learn to be suspicious of premature consensus and either/or thinking. Peter Drucker declared provocatively : 'The first rule in decision making is that one does not make a decision unless there is disagreement,' and he illustrated his point with this story :

Albert P. Sloan [former head of General Motors] is reported to have said at a meeting of one of his top committees : 'Gentlemen, I take it we are all in complete agreement on the decision here.' Everyone around the table nodded assent. 'Then,' continued Mr Sloan, 'I propose we postpone further discussion of this matter until our next meeting to give ourselves time to develop disagreement and perhaps gain some understanding of what the decision is all about.'[4]

Von Moltke, the famous German strategist, once remarked : 'If you think your enemy has two courses open to him, be sure that he will chose the third.' Wise leaders seek to proliferate courses of action. They keep the span of their attention at wide focus, so that they receive most light from the situation, before narrowing down the focus of their minds. Other people of committees can be useful here, for every individual has a slightly different viewpoint. Some people can see round the 'hill of difficulty' which closes or restricts our own field of vision, and suggest courses of action that would not have occurred to us.

Peter Drucker also made the useful point that one possible course almost always involves taking no decision at all :

> To take no decision is a decision as fully as to take specific action. The danger is that we may simply drift into that possibility in the hopes of avoiding all unpleasant consequences. Only by judging the consequences of doing nothing can we transform it into a possible course of action. Decisions are like surgery, carrying with them all the setting up of all kinds of chain reactions in the living organisms of relationships, organizations and societies. Even if the decision is a minor one it can always cause a mild degree of shock. Sometimes the organism might survive the shock and benefit from the surgical operation; at other times a decision might finish it off. In the latter case the remedy can be worse than the disease.[5]

MAKING THE DECISION

The analytical, synthetic and valuing (or critical) methods of thinking then get to work exploring and weighing the different courses of action. The facets of doing this are : listing the advantages and disadvantages; examining the consequences of each course; measuring against standards, criteria and values; testing beside the yardstick of the aim or objective; weighing the risks against the expected gains.

Obviously these considerations overlap, and the differences between them are partly semantic. But the major intellectual activity at this point is valuing. Sometimes, where the only relevant criteria are quantifiable, the decision may be easily reached. A decision is a course of action which is chosen in such a way that the thinking process is 'cut off' and we stop seriously considering the other possibilities. If the background and foreground intellectual work has been done properly, the mind should move through this phase as simply and smoothly as a turning wheel passing its zenith.

Clearly it helps if the criteria or ground rules for the decision are thought out in advance. Generally speaking there is rarely one single criterion against which a possible course can be measured : we have to rely upon a number of criteria. Management is the art of maximizing a number of variables, not just one or two. Even an apparently simple criterion like 'profit' needs careful analysis.

Sir Arnold Weinstock, Chairman of General Electric, has been reported as employing seven key business ratios as a guide to management (which could also be used for assessing courses of action for the future with the word 'expected' placed in front of them). These ratios are : profits/capital employed; profits/sales; sales/capital employed; sales/fixed assets; sales/stocks; sales per employee; profits per employee.

Needless to say such terms as 'stocks' would require careful definition. It could also be argued that the concept of 'profitability' is not exhausted by this list. For instance, we would need to consider the ratio between output and capacity. Useful tools though they are, such ratios and formulas cannot ever replace the need for managerial judgement.[6]

Again the depth mind can be most important in this phase of the decision-making process. We all know the benefits of 'sleeping on it', thereby allowing the depth mind to do its work. The depth mind sometimes seems to be able to take account of the missing information, the gaps in our knowledge, the interrelations of factors and courses of action matched against deep moral and personal values, and then to suggest to us the right decision. Many people find that the practice of setting a date or time limit for the decision concentrates the depth mind for the final phase of its work.

When the depth mind has carried out its computer-like calculations in the 10,000 million cells of the brain, it offers the decision : not neatly typed on a piece of paper, but by giving more weight to one course of action over the others. This requires a certain sensitivity to the workings of the depth mind. The relevant attitude or posture of the surface to the depth mind at this stage has been well described by the philosopher Simone Weil :

Attention consists of suspending our thought, leaving it detached, empty and ready to be penetrated by the object, it means holding in our minds, within reach of this thought, but on a lower level and not in contact with it, the diverse knowledge we have acquired which we are forced to make use of. Our thoughts should be in relation to all particular and already formulated thoughts, as a man on a mountain who, as he looks forward, sees also below him, without actually looking at them, a great many forests and plains. Above all our thought should be empty, waiting, not seeking anything, but ready to receive in its naked truth the object which is to penetrate it.

All wrong translations, all absurdities in geometry problems, all clumsiness of style and all faulty connection of ideas in compositions and essays, all such things are due to the fact that thought has seized upon some idea too hastily and being thus prematurely blocked, is not open to the truth. The cause is always that we have wanted to be too active; we have wanted to carry out a search. This can be proved every time, for every fault, if we trace it to its root. There is no better exercise than such a tracing down of our faults, for this truth is one of those which we can only believe when we have experienced it hundreds and thousands of times. This is the way with all essential truths.[7]

IMPLEMENTING THE DECISION

The act of decision may take place anywhere in the continuum of the surface and depth minds, but the process is not complete until it is implemented and we have learnt to live with the consequences. Decisions are often lost at this point and resolute choice gives way to wavering indecision. The reason for this phenomenon is that all decisions are a 'cutting off' or amputation of the thinking process. Sometimes the wound is clean and painless, the scars heal and the decision bears fruit. In other cases the cutting off takes place effectively only in the surface mind: the rejected possibilities linger on in the depth mind, waiting their chance to appeal again in a higher court when occasion allows.

The re-emergence of a rejected possibility often coincides with vigorous criticism of the decision that has actually been made. This can be a testing experience for a leader, for he must tread the tightrope between inflexibility and rigidity on the one hand, and indecisiveness on the other hand. Once he entertains a serious doubt about his decision the leader falls into a dilemma. 'A foolish consistency is the hobgoblin of little minds,' wrote Emerson. Every leader hopes that he is flexible enough to change his mind if necessary or that he has sufficient humility to admit that he is mistaken or wrong. On the other hand, most managers fear being thought weak or indecisive and this may close their minds as tight as a Chinese puzzle.

In the Eisenhower case study (p. 33) there is a possible solution to the dilemma. The leader should indeed be prepared to reconsider his decision, but only if he weighs the proposed change against the consequences of changing his mind. 'Changing horses in mid-stream', as the well-worn phrase has it, is a hazardous manoeuvre, quite different from judging the suitability of the two mounts when they stand meekly upon the river bank. Among the consequences, besides the syndrome of 'order–counter-order–disorder', there may be a fall in the leader's popularity. Moreover, trust is linked to consistency and respect to firmness in maintaining a decision. But there are cases where a wrong decision has been reached through a miscalculation, and if there is still time the leader has to change course and face the consequences, both corporate and personal.

Therefore there is a point of no return between the time when the decision has been made and the moment when the commitment to it is judged to be irrevocable in terms of consequences. Before this important moment the decision maker can to a certain extent experience the feel of the decision as an actuality, knowing at the back of his mind that he has leeway to change to another decision, if new evidence demands it, before he has passed the point of no return.

Deciding where the point of no return lies can be an important decision in its own right. Unlike air flights, it does not necessarily occur at a middle point. A working definition of it would be : 'the last point when you can make a change without causing confusion in terms of the completion of the aim and the people involved'. Responsibility for a decision includes responsibility for changing it up to the point of no return. This does not mean, however, that a decision which is adequate and able to achieve the aim should be abandoned because a better course of action suddenly presents itself. Only if new factors weigh heavily against the feasibility of the adopted decision should another course be seriously considered. Once one is committed, beyond the no return point, new factors or proposals cannot by definition result in any change of course.

A corollary is that one should not commit oneself prematurely to a statement or position, as Alice found to her cost in *Through the Looking Glass*.

'The cause of lightning,' said Alice very decidedly, for she felt sure about this, 'is thunder – no, no !' she hastily corrected herself, 'I meant the other way.'

'It's too late to correct it,' said the Red Queen. 'When you've once said a thing, that fixes it, and you must take the consequences.'[8]

Most text-books advocate that we should weigh the consequences of our decision in advance, but they ignore the fact that not all the consequences can be foreseen. We may conveniently distinguish between manifest and latent consequences, the former being those evident upon examination, and the latter unforeseen. For example, it was not evident that the building of the Aswan Dam in Egypt would lead to the death of a certain species of fish in the Mediterrannean (by cutting down the flow of fresh water into the sea). Most decisions need corrective decisions to deal with such unforeseen or latent consequences, just as a car driver who corners to the right soon has to turn the steering wheel over to the left to come on course again.

The pressures which the decision maker can be subjected to (both from within and without) in the time between the act or moment of decision and the point of no return mount in ratio with the importance or gravity of the decision. The more costly an error the more potential pressure the decision maker may experience, and the more he will need to be clear and firm in his judgement. Often a leader's calmness and confidence, his ability to keep his head while others about him are 'losing theirs and blaming it on him', will help to create the climate in which the decision, possibly not the best one, can yet be effectively implemented.

Decision-making models

Observations of actual decision-making and problem-solving behaviour support the above theoretical contention that the human mind does not naturally follow the neat, logical and sequential analysis usually recommended in the text-books. Rather our thinking tends to be often untidy and illogical, with the phases being tried in turns which vary like musical notes in a scale.[9]

In an American attempt to study how decisions are made in

real life as opposed to the psychologists' laboratories, Nicholas Nicolaidis analysed 332 administrative decisions made by public officials.[10] Far from decisions being based purely on rational reasons, he found strong admixtures of emotions, power politics, the influences of other people and the individual decision maker's own values. Instead of following classic steps in which ends and means are distinguished, all the possible facts and factors gathered and weighed, alternative courses or solutions advanced and the most rational one (in terms of such criteria as expected consequences) chosen, he found that facts, values, ends and means were confused. Owing to the limitations of the human mind, shortage of time, defective or inadequate communications systems and the confusion of facts and values, many decisions rested upon very incomplete information and the course selected was only one of a limited and incomplete number available. Finally, though decision makers applied reason to their decisions, they also introduced their own values and often some organizational politics, and then, to make the decision seem objective and rational, they claimed it was for the good of the organization!

Moreover, the decision makers rarely settled for the best or optimum solution as recommended by the management text-books, but tended to look for a satisfactory compromise among two or more of the courses or solutions, i.e. one that :

(i) agreed, at least to some extent, with their own personal interests, values and needs;

(ii) met the value standards of their supervisors;

(iii) was acceptable to both those who would be affected by the decision and those who had to carry it out;

(iv) looked reasonable in its context;

(v) contained a built-in justification which would furnish an excuse, and possibly an avenue of retreat, in case the actual results of the decision turned out to be quite different from those anticipated.

Nicolaidis concluded that the 'real' decision makers tended to reach decisions by muddling through with a concern for deciding promptly and with the least uncertainty. In almost all cases other people were consulted or involved, and the resulting decision was a compromise which would be acceptable to as wide a spectrum of the people concerned as possible.

Peter Drucker graphically and simply distinguished between two different kinds of compromise :

One kind is expressed in the old proverb; 'Half a loaf is better than no bread.' The other kind is expressed in the story of the Judgement of Solomon, which was clearly based on the realization that 'half a baby is worse than no baby at all.' In the first instance, the boundary conditions are still being satisfied. The purpose of bread is to provide food, and half a loaf is still food. Half a baby, however, does not satisfy the boundary conditions. For half a baby is not half of a living and growing child. It is a corpse in two pieces.[11]

The foregoing summary of the study by Nicolaidis may have first suggested to the reader that leaders in industry, commerce and the public services could do with some improvements in their decision-making approaches; and, secondly, that the sequential, rational or logical methods of deciding or solving problems so tirelessly recommended to them in management literature could also do with a great deal of attention. As models they bear too little relation to what actually happens in working situations.

One theme of this book is that such a classification is unnecessary if we go back to the nature of thinking. Here, analysis, synthesis and value-thinking co-exist naturally together. The everchanging colour patterns or musical harmonies of these three themes make up the observable part of applied thinking. Below the surface mind we have postulated a depth mind which plays perhaps the largest part in all our thinking. Moreover, we have early recognized that there is no final dichotomy between reason and emotion : even rigorous analytical thinking has its pleasures and pains, although it may take a sensitive palate to taste them.

We must now turn to the social dimension of decision making. For so far we have looked upon the decision maker as an individual, like Rodin's statue *The Thinker*; now we must set him in the context of the people in an organization or society with whom and for whom he is deciding. For other people play an important part in the thinking process, both indirectly and directly, as we shall see in the next chapter.

CHAPTER FOUR

SHARING DECISIONS

Into the minds of leaders in any sphere of life there must enter a constant question : 'How far should I share my decisions with other members of the group or organization?' Any book on decision making today would be incomplete if it treated the process purely as an intellectual exercise by the leader which did not involve other people. The subject of this chapter is the social dimension of decision making, problem solving and creative thinking.

Certainly the pressures that are on managers to share decisions are considerable. There seems to be a general if uneven desire throughout the world for greater participation, and that means participation in the decisions which affect the working lives of those concerned, be they factory workers or university students. How far should people share in decisions within industry or any other *milieu* of leadership?

In a thoughtful and most influential article called 'How to Choose a Leadership Pattern' in the *Harvard Business Review,* two Americans, Robert Tannenbaum and Warren H. Schmidt, addressed themselves to this fundamental question.[1] First they pointed out that the leader's natural dilemma had been heightened by the effects of 'group dynamics' laboratories :

Through training laboratories in group development that sprang up across the country, many of the newer notions of leadership began to exert an impact. These training laboratories were carefully designed to give people a first-hand experience in full participation and decision making. The designated 'leaders' deliberately attempted to reduce their own power and to make group members as responsible as possible for setting their own goals and methods within the laboratory experience.

It was perhaps inevitable that some of the people who attended the training laboratories regarded this kind of leadership as being truly 'democratic' and went home with the determination to build fully participative decision making into their own organizations. Whenever their bosses made a decision without convening a staff meeting, they tended to perceive this as authoritarian behavior. The true symbol of democratic leadership to some was the meeting – and the less directed from the top, the more democratic it was.

Some of the more enthusiastic alumni of these training laboratories began to get the habit of categorizing leader behavior as 'democratic' or 'authoritarian'. The boss who made too many decisions himself was thought of as an authoritarian, and his directive behavior was often attributed solely to his personality.

Clearly words like 'autocratic', 'authoritarian', 'democratic' and 'permissive', when applied to decision making, carry with them overtones of moral judgement. Freeing ourselves for a moment from any such preconceptions let us consider the 'continuum of leadership behaviour', the possible range of sharing decisions, which the two authors present. They visualized a decision as being like a cake which could be divided up in several ways by leader and subordinates :

Let us look briefly at each of the 'decision points' from left to right of the continuum :

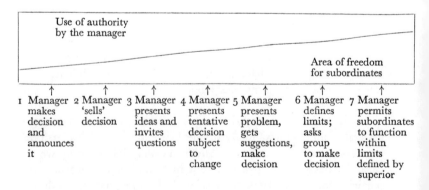

| 1 Manager makes decision and announces it | 2 Manager 'sells' decision | 3 Manager presents ideas and invites questions | 4 Manager presents tentative decision subject to change | 5 Manager presents problem, gets suggestions, make decision | 6 Manager defines limits; asks group to make decision | 7 Manager permits subordinates to function within limits defined by superior |

I MANAGER MAKES DECISION AND ANNOUNCES IT

Having reviewed the 'courses of action' in the light of the aim or objective and the prevailing factors the manager selects one course and tells his subordinates his decision. How they will react may have come into his calculations, but they have no direct share in the decision-making process.

2 MANAGER MAKES DECISION AND 'SELLS' IT

Here the manager makes the decision, announces it and goes on to give the reasons for it, and to state the advantages that accrue from it to the subordinates. Implicitly he is recognizing their importance in implementing the decision.

3 MANAGER PRESENTS IDEAS AND INVITES QUESTIONS

The manager presents some of the background thinking behind the decision – for example the factors and the courses open. He asks for questions so that the subordinates can truly enter into the decision, explore it and accept it. The discussion allows all concerned to become clearer about the implications of decision.

4 MANAGER PRESENTS A TENTATIVE DECISION SUBJECT TO CHANGE

The proposed decision is offered for discussion and review. Having heard the comments and questions from those who will be affected by it, the manager reserves for himself the final decision.

5 MANAGER PRESENTS PROBLEM, GETS SUGGESTIONS, THEN DECIDES

The manager identifies the problem or the option of courses of action which lead towards the goal, and comes before the subordinates without his mind being weighted towards any one solution or plan. The function of the group becomes one of increasing the manager's repertory of possible solutions to the problem. The purpose is to capitalize on the knowledge and experience of those who are on the 'firing line'. From the expanded list of alternatives developed by the manager and his subordinates, the manager then selects the solution that he regards as most promising.

6 MANAGER DEFINES LIMITS, ASKS GROUP TO DECIDE

At this point the manager hands over the decision to the group (which may be held to include himself), having spelt out the choice that must be made and the boundaries or limits which the decision must respect, including the financial restrictions.

7 MANAGER PERMITS GROUP TO DECIDE WITHIN PRESCRIBED LIMITS

This represents an extreme degree of group freedom only occasionally encountered in formal organizations, as, for instance, in many research groups. Here the team of managers or engineers undertakes the identification and diagnosis of the problem, develops alternative procedures for solving it, and decides on one or more of these alternative solutions. The only limits directly imposed on the group by the organization are those specified by the superior or the team's boss. If the boss participates in the decision-making process, he attempts to do so with no more authority than any other member of the group. He commits himself in advance to assist in implementing whatever decision the group makes.

Using the continuum

As we have noted, varying pressures are upon all leaders to move steadily or precipitately towards the right-hand edge of the scale. There are some good reasons why they should let this particular wind of change fill their sails. For example, we know that the more people share in decisions which affect their working lives the more they are motivated to carry them out. This important truth is one of the main foundations of the modern practice of 'management by objectives', the discipline of sitting down and agreeing objectives with subordinates. Nor is it simply a gimmick : one can know all about it and still appreciate an opportunity for genuine participation.[2]

That being so, what are the factors which hold back the leader from moving to the right of the continuum? Tannenbaum and Schmidt recognize three factors or forces of particular importance : forces in the manager; forces in the subordinates; forces in the situation. We can use this three-fold analysis either to gain a better understanding of past decisions in a group or organization, or as an exploration of the key factors a leader or manager must balance in his conscious (and depth) mind when making a decision.

The manager

Among the factors or forces within the leader (or manager in the industrial or commercial situations) are his own values. What is his 'doctrine of man'? Secondly, he brings with him a certain personality which may include a bias towards one end of the scale rather than the other. He may feel more comfortable in one range of the continuum rather than the other, just as Mozart felt happier composing in some keys rather than others. He may have a low 'tolerance for ambiguity' which drives him to be inappropriately directive. On the other hand he may have a 'people-centred' bias which leads him to dissipate his own decision-making responsibility.

Given a modicum of self-understanding the good leader is able to recognize, allow for and discount if necessary the forces he carries within him, personal prejudices which draw him magnetically towards set patterns or syndromes of behaviour. While aware of his own experience, strengths and weaknesses he is still prepared to treat each day as a new one. For a weakness is only a tendency to act in a certain way under pressure. Effective leaders seem to choose the *milieu* where their natural style of decision making fits most appropriately, and then learn the necessary variations.

The subordinates

The second key factor is the subordinates. What knowledge and experience do they possess? Are they qualified or competent in any way to contribute to the decision? Clearly there is a great deal of difference between making a managerial decision where none of those present has any knowledge or background relevant to the matter in hand, and making one where all concerned are both experienced and competent. For this reason the higher the level of decisions in organizations the more they tend towards the right-hand of the continuum. The British Cabinet, for example, composed of heads of government departments and other senior ministers, would usually endeavour to reach consensus; even voting on important issues is extremely rare.[3] Paradoxically, the American Constitution reserves much greater decision-making power to one man – the President. For example, when Abraham Lincoln convened his Cabinet to read them the Emancipation Proclamation, he prefaced it with these words: 'I have gathered you together to hear what I have written down. I do not seek your advice about the main matter ... that I have determined for myself.'[4]

Another important factor under this general heading is the expectations of the subordinates: do they expect to be told or to be consulted? To some extent this relates to what they have become accustomed to in the past, and whether to respect the expectation or to seek to change it, either in one specific instance or permanently, can often be a major leadership decision in itself.

Forces in the situation

A third key factor is the situation. In organizations or groups which work characteristically in crisis situations, i.e. ones in which by definition time is in very short supply and where (often) there is a life-or-death dimension, leaders tend to make decisions and announce them. Moreover, as research at the scenes of road accidents and forest fires reveals, people expect firm and definite leadership from one man – they need it. For this reason, para-doxically, it is easier for the army officer to lead soldiers on active service than in peacetime.

I mention and emphasize the time factor first here, because it strikes me as being the key one, but Tannenbaum and Schmidt place it fourth and deal with it only very superficially. Under this heading the authors of *The Harvard Business Review* first place the values and traditions of the employing body : what could be called the organizational situation or setting. As Douglas McGregor powerfully suggests, organizations can differ widely in their corpor-ate philosophies, especially in their views of mankind, the nature of human relations and the roles of leaders and subordinates.[5] Factors such as the wide geographical dispersion of an organization might militate against a high degree of participation, or a need for security might limit the extent to which a manager can divulge confidential information. Moreover, beyond the organization lies the wider social environment, the given culture with its fixed norms and changing standards.

The authors also briefly suggested, under the heading 'The Problem Itself', that the actual problem was a 'force in the situa-tion', noting that the very complexity and specialized nature of many problems may make it easier for the manager to tackle it himself, rather than to occupy his staff for the amount of time needed to give them all the background information and relevant data. 'The key question to ask, of course, is : "Have I heard the ideas of everyone who has the necessary knowledge to make a significant contribution to the solution of this problem?" '

'Thus, the successful manager of men can be primarily charac-terized neither as a strong leader nor a permissive one,' the two authors conclude. 'Rather he is one who maintains a high batting average in accurately assessing the forces that determine what his most appropriate behavior at any given time should be and in actually being able to behave accordingly. Being both insightful and flexible, he is less likely to see the problems of leadership as a dilemma.'

Within the context of this book we might add that the authors of 'How to Choose a Leadership Pattern' show a confusion between decision making and problem solving, at least in the language they use. Managers hearing an exposition of the article are swift to point out that the complexity of the problem is not the only factor in question when one comes to decision making. In the distinction between ends and means it may be impossible to allow groups or individual subordinates share in decision about purpose, aims or even objectives (in some organizations), but more often than not there is endless room for participation in decisions over the means or methods to be adopted.

Norman R. F. Maier, Professor of Psychology at the University of Michigan, has usefully suggested a three-fold classification of problems or decisions (he did not distinguish between them), taking into account what could be called the 'people dimension' which is so often left out of the picture altogether by most books with the words 'decision making' in their titles.[6]

HIGH-QUALITY, LOW-ACCEPTANCE REQUIREMENT

This is characteristic of decisions in which the quality of the decision is an important ingredient and the need for acceptance is relatively low. The acceptance factor should come up for consideration only after the leader has satisfied himself that he has made the right decision. Not unlike Tannenbaum and Schmidt in the article summarized above, Professor Maier seems to regard these as the expert, specialized or complex decisions, such as those concerning expansion, new products, decentralization, plant sites, setting prices, purchase of materials and the solution of technical problems. Maier allows, however, that there is room for disagreement on what constitutes the quality and acceptance requirements of a decision, and declares : 'This evaluation must be made by the person who is responsible for the decision.' In the British industrial relations situation we might add that the trades unions might have a valuable part to play in exploring the distinction at depth.

HIGH-ACCEPTANCE, LOW-QUALITY REQUIREMENT

These are decisions in which poor acceptance can cause failure and in which the judgement of quality, according to Professor Maier, 'is influenced by differences in position, experience, attitudes, value systems, and other subjective factors'. Such decisions, he holds, are best made by the group, and he quotes the example of a supervisor wanting two out of three girls to work overtime and leaving to them the decision of which two. Such high-acceptance decisions are particularly relevant in matters involving fairness, such as :

(i) the fair way to distribute anything desirable, e.g. food, equipment, vehicles, tools, office space or furniture;

(ii) the fair way to get something undesirable done, e.g. unpleasant work, unattractive hours or shifts;

(iii) the timing of holidays, overtime, coffee- or tea-breaks etc.;

(iv) the fair way to settle disciplinary problems that involve violations of regulations, lack of co-operation etc.

Although we may cavil at the last of Professor Maier's categories, his general point stands.

HIGH-ACCEPTANCE, HIGH-QUALITY REQUIREMENT

Professor Maier defined this group rather negatively as the decisions that do not fall into the other two categories and gave no examples. He contented himself with giving the reassurance that 'group decisions are often of surprisingly good quality.'[7]

We might add that the continuum on page 66 suggests that there are more ways than group decision of gaining high acceptance. For if people contribute ideas or suggestions, if (in a word) they are consulted, they will tend to accept the eventual decision – providing that they believe that their advice has been genuinely listened to and heeded, and not sought as a matter of form, because some text-book or management course has told the leader in question that it is a 'good thing' to go through this particular routine.

Some further key questions on sharing decisions

Leaders in industry, commerce, public service and the armed services have raised some important questions in discussions with the author about the Tannenbaum and Schmidt continuum :

WHAT HAPPENS TO A LEADER'S RESPONSIBILITY WHEN HE SHARES DECISIONS?

My view, shared with the authors of the article, is that if the leader delegates a decision to a group or an individual (for the continuum holds good if there are only two people involved) he still remains ultimately responsible for the quality of the decision.

He cannot pass the buck. He has to accept the risks as well as the advantages involved in delegation.

DOES CONSISTENCY MATTER MORE THAN ANY OTHER FACTOR?

There is one British research study which suggests that 'leaders who are seen as having distinct and identifiable styles of leadership are more effective in promoting confidence and satisfaction, *whatever style they adopt*, than those who do not have a distinctive style. This suggests that one important characteristic of the successful leader is consistency of behaviour, which enables subordinates to know where they stand with him and to predict his actions and reactions.'[8] But there is a difference between inflexibility and consistency. The leader can be consistent, for example, in always making it clear in any given instance just where he intends the decision to be taken in terms of the scale. There are times also when leaders must shatter people's expectations; in these moments leaders may have to face and overcome their own fear of being judged inconsistent by others.

IS IT BETTER TO BE A DEMOCRATIC RATHER THAN AN AUTHORITARIAN LEADER?

These are value-judgements imported into the field. It gets you nowhere to label different points on the scale as '*laissez-faire*' or 'autocratic'. A fire chief officer ordering his men about in a blazing hospital should not be accused of being autocratic. Nor should an educational leader making his or her students think for themselves be described as '*laissez-faire*'. In particular, 'democratic' and 'autocratic' are political terms which may become the equivalents of the moral words 'good' and 'bad' when applied consciously or unconsciously to managers in the worlds of industry and the public services. The degree of decision sharing should be appropriate only in terms of the situation. In its wider contexts, that situation will include the political and social values of the given culture, but these cannot be in the foreground. There is a morality in leadership and decision making, but it is not necessarily inherent in the degree of participation of the subordinates in the process. Nor should participation be confused with democracy.

Norms of shared decision making

In the people dimension of applied thinking there are three clusters of factors to be considered: the leader himself, the group and the situation. For the guidance of leaders and followers we can chart the possibilities of sharing decisions openly, thereby revealing that there are several routes to genuine participation other than simple group decision.

By a consideration of the factors in the general environment of industry today it would seem that within the full spectrum of the scale open to the leaders there are optimum levels, like the boiling and freezing points on a thermometer. In the light of their experience of 'management by objectives' and the powers (or dynamics) latent in good teams, which are often unleashed by participation, few leaders would want to make and announce all decisions themselves, despite their need to exercise this authority in some of the characteristic situations which make up their total working environment.

On the other hand, the widespread assumption that only democratic decisions (made by majority vote or consensus) are good ones in the moral sense, has been increasingly challenged on both sides of the Atlantic. American theorists in this field should have been warned long ago against this false conclusion by the honest words of the eminent Professor Douglas McGregor, author of the widely influential book *The Human Side of Enterprise,* who became a college president in 1948 after years as a teacher at the Massachusetts Institute of Technology :

> It took the direct experience of becoming a line executive, and meeting personally the problems involved, to teach me what no amount of observation of other people could have taught.
>
> I believed, for example, that a leader could operate successfully as a kind of adviser to his organization. I thought I could avoid being a 'boss'. Unconsciously, I suspect, I hoped to duck the unpleasant necessity of making difficult decisions, of taking the responsibility for one course of action among many uncertain alternatives, of making mistakes and taking the consequences. I thought that maybe I could operate so that everyone would like me – that 'good human relations' would eliminate all discord and disagreement.
>
> I could not have been more wrong. It took a couple of years, but I finally began to realize that a leader cannot avoid the exercise of authority any more than he can avoid responsibility for what happens to his organization. In fact, it is a major function of the top executive to take on his own shoulders the

responsibility for resolving the uncertainties that are always involved in important decisions. Moreover, since no important decision ever pleases everyone in the organization, he must also absorb the displeasure, and sometimes severe hostility, of those who would have taken a different course.[9]

Managers may well be right to set one end of their own decision making span short of full group decision. In 1969, Lord Cole, then Chairman of Unilever, aptly expressed this viewpoint in a speech at the annual general meeting of the firm :

> You may feel that Unilever is rather like a Parliamentary democracy. This is not so. But it is true that ours is a company in which, much more than in most, a value is placed on every manager's contribution. I am not talking about worker participation which is a separate and complex subject. Nor do I claim that we achieve full managerial participation. That is very difficult to achieve even if it were desirable, and if only because it is so time-consuming : sometimes the need for speed or security or both does not permit consultation. A testing of the temperature is all that is possible. But we do believe that in a world where people demand more and more to have a share in the decisions which govern their working lives and to be able to contribute to them any creativity they themselves may have, the Unilever style of management is going to be an increasing asset.

Thus a management approach begins to emerge where there is consultation, and as much participation as the situation allows; but the leader normally reserves to himself the actual making of the decision. What he cannot avoid, however, in all his decisions, is the 'people dimension', and it has been the object of this chapter so far to explore what that responsibility involves.

CONTRIBUTING NEW IDEAS

Lord Cole's mention of 'creativity' in relation to decision making illustrates a growing concern in industry that all the natural resources available should be tapped, including the most precious and rare resource of all – the creativity of the human mind. Later in this book we shall look more deeply into the nature of creativity and also review current training programmes in creative thinking. At this point, however, it is relevant to state that people in enterprises have as much to contribute to creative thinking and problem solving as they do to decision making. To a large extent the production of new ideas can be a social process, influenced by the organizational climate and directly encouraged by management.

In one basic form this approach was pioneered in Britain under the title of 'Suggestions Schemes'.[10] For a number of years the Industrial Society (formerly the Industrial Welfare Society) acted as a central co-ordinator, giving advice on appropriate posters and financial rewards. In the United States the scheme has been elaborated into a system, with a philosophy attached to it. The version taught by Dr C. C. Drawford of the University of Southern California is called 'systematized directed induction'. Here is an account of its operation by Mary Bosticco, which appeared in *The Times* of 30 December, 1968 :

Scudder Food Products Inc., a potato crisp manufacturer with several branches in California, wants guidance on improving operations and increasing its prosperity. It calls in consultants who bring together all Scudder's available executives, a large number of their supervisors, and a cross-section of the staff, including some of the roundsmen, who make deliveries by van. In all, 140 people are surveyed, in eight workshop sessions. As they sit, four to a table, the conferees are told the management is anxious to improve operations and increase company prosperity and is asking for their help. Obvious there are difficulties, obstacles in the way to greater success. What are these obstacles in the eyes of the conferees? Will they please write them down, each problem on one of the small slips of paper provided. The problem-statement slips have the words 'How to . . .' printed on them and participants state the problems by completing the sentence.

Participants are coaxed into giving the problem statements considerable thought and to spend several minutes in discussion with their table partners. Finally, when every problem is thoroughly thrashed out and set down, participants are asked to rate the four most important ones.

This part of the exercise is extremely important since it brings to light every difficulty from every department. Once stated, the problem is half solved, as is well known.

Participants are then asked how they would solve their four problems. Solutions are written on differently coloured slips, one per idea. Solution slips are clipped to their respective problem slips and handed to the consultants. At no point are participants asked to identify their slips in any way – every contribution remains anonymous.

I do not recall how many pink and green slips we took back to the office that afternoon, but there were well over 2,000. My task was to sort and organize them and then create a synthesis out of that brainpool of ideas.

Gradually, as I pored over the piles of small slips, an image of Scudder Foods Inc. formed before my eyes: a company needing to clarify its organization chart and form well-defined lines of authority; to install a supervisory and sales training programme; to improve its product planning and quality control; to reorganize its paperwork; to improve communications throughout; a company which, in spite of its apparent short-comings, was well loved by its staff, who were anxious to welcome new and better methods. There were suggestions on how to improve the product, minimize waste, reduce accidents in the plant, increase cleanliness, both of plant and product, and much more. The section on selling alone was an embryo sales manual!

I don't know how many of the suggestions were implemented by the management. Certainly a sales training programme was established and the company went from strength to strength.

Similar surveys were carried out for such diverse companies as General Telephone and Electronics, the second largest American telephone company, which was decentralizing, the Marquardt Aircraft Corp. and Mattel Inc., the toy manufacturers.

Perhaps one day British companies will realize an untapped vein of creativity lies fallow in their midst.

In the United Kingdom in 1970 it is estimated that six hundred firms have suggestions schemes, an advance of only one hundred or so on the total number ten years ago. Yet recently Morgan Crucible Ltd paid £4,800 to an employee for a valuable suggestion that cut down rejects from ten per cent to nil, the largest sum ever awarded outside the United States. The Ford Motor Company offers up to £1,000 and a free new car to its employees for ideas that are of significant help, and such prizes are often awarded several times a month.

Thus from both British and American experience, not to mention the benefits from suggestions schemes reported in Western Europe and Russia, it is clear that people working at all levels of industry may well have valuable practical suggestions and fresh ideas to contribute towards the central or corporate thinking of an enterprise. But this fact does not take us outside the framework of reference outlined by Tannenbaum and Schmidt; rather it extends our vision of the resources other than specialized skills or technical knowledge which are present in the minds of all concerned. Now we must turn to a more specialized aspect of a manager's mental activity : problem solving.

CHAPTER FIVE

PROBLEM SOLVING

The word 'problem' is sufficiently general in its meaning to lend itself to a wide interpretation. We talk, for example, about a 'problem child', the problem of world peace, problems in science, mathematics and the arts, and the daily problems facing a manager. Obviously a word that is used so widely needs careful definition by anyone bold enough to employ it.

As mention earlier in Chapter One, 'problem' derives from the Greek word *problema*, literally 'a thing thrown or put forward'. The second part of the word comes from a root that gives us also 'ball' and 'ballistics'. Probably the earliest 'thing' thrown or put forward was a question for academic discussion or scholarly disputation, and the word has never quite lost an academic flavour owing to this parentage, as its frequent and specialized uses in the field of logic, geometry, physics, mathematics and chess testify.

This linguistic history has tended – consciously or unconsciously – to make managers and other practically-minded decision makers rather suspicious of problem solving. Their hesitation often arises from an awareness that problem solving and decision making, although superficially they overlap so much both in subject matter and in methods of approach, in fact require different orders of mind, heart and soul. Academic problems, for example, tend to be presented in a theoretical way in a limited environment. In other words, the problem is put to you in such a way that it is capable of solution in terms of given (or easily acquired) information; there are clear limits around the problem, like a fence round a house. The word problem also has academic overtones in that its existence or solution does not really affect the environment in which it is presented. The solution of the problem is an end in itself, and not a means towards some other end.

The contrast between problems of everyday personal or professional life and academic ones is at once obvious. Indeed, in the strict sense of the term, often the only problems a manager solves are those contained in the crossword puzzle that he might tackle on the train going to work! The problems that really concern us are open in that we often do not have all the information needed to find the best solution. Moreover, the problems are alive in that the way we handle them can influence both us and our environment. Very few of us seek out or invent such problems in order to solve them for the intellectual fun of it (which is not the same as saying that people do not enjoy – secretly or openly – having problems, and the challenging stimulus they bring to their lives).

However, the difference between academic problem solving and practical decision making is always in danger of yawning into yet another false dichotomy. One only has to reflect upon the exasperated comments of many senior managers upon the academic teachers of management in the universities and business schools, or the equally annoying air of Olympian condescension adopted by some academics, to see the force of this point.

What is the relation between problem solving and decision making, if we reject the view that they are totally distinct in every way?

Take the case of Napoleon. The biographer of the fallen emperor's last years on St Helena informs us that Napoleon invariably lost when he played chess: he made his moves too fast and he cheated shamelessly.[1] Now chess has the marks of being an ancient Chinese war game in origin, and so we have the interesting spectacle of perhaps the greatest battle-winner in history consistently failing to perform winning manoeuvres on the chessboard.

Confronted with this piece of evidence, it would be easy to jump to the conclusion that Napoleon's failure proves that problem solving has nothing whatsoever to do with decision making; that in the heat and confusion of battle, Napoleon excelled in the arts of summing up situations, making swift decisions on inadequate evidence and managing the movements of corps and divisions which he had previously successfully organized into armies. In the 'open' situation of real life, where speed of decision might matter more than a slow laborious computation of all the possibilities, surely Napoleon had proved his worth. On the other hand, while freely admitting that chess may not reveal certain qualities of the true decision maker, it is quite possible that there was a relation or an overlap between the way in which Napoleon played chess against his aides and his battles with opposing generals. Many of his early victories, for example, were won by getting there 'fastest with the mostest', combined with the high morale of his armies. He excelled also at battles on the move, the highly mobile march-and-fight campaigns. At Waterloo, however, where he was much more in the chessboard situation, it could be argued that his defeat – so often blamed on illness, incompetent subordinates or bad luck – sprang from moving his pieces swiftly but thoughtlessly, relying on *panache* rather than a cool assessment of the possibilities. So much so that when he came to play his queen, the Old Guard, the game was already lost.

Only the existence of this kind of relationship between problem solving and decision making can justify the use of case-studies and practical exercises in management education. For a case-study is a linear descendant of the problems posed to the Greek philosophers. Like modern war games, it has been couched in a conceptual framework more relevant to the decision-making life of the student than the chessboard. Yet it remains a theoretical problem in a limited environment, however much real life is simulated in time/space terms. An army on training manoeuvres is still problem solving; real war is somewhere else on the almost completely different scale of decision making. Yet if there was no possible 'transfer' from one to the other situation, there would be no point in problem, case-study or manoeuvre.

We must therefore firmly reject the idea that problem solving and decision making are so far apart that ne'er the twain shall meet. The two are alike and different at the same time. Having explored the obvious differences, it is now time to look at the similarities, and to delineate the position that I believe that problem solving should occupy in relation to the decision making described in the last chapter.

Problem solving and decision making

Psychologically it could be said that 'a thing thrown or put forward' becomes a problem to me only if I am aware of the 'thing' as an obstacle between myself and the end I want to gain. In other words, I become aware of a problem only when I have a prior awareness of some objective, aim or purpose that I am seeking to accomplish. If I want to get from London to New York urgently by a certain time, I have no problem if I can get there by some simple method. But I soon become aware of a problem if my flight is cancelled or there is a dock strike. Now most problems in the conventional or academic sense either assume and expect you to accept some implicit or explicit aim and then tease you by creating an artificial problem state (e.g. games such as chess); or else they are really questions which become problems only in the psychological sense because they are obstacles to some external end the subject is seeking. For example, a riddle becomes a problem only to those who have some ulterior motive for wanting to answer it; hence the diligence of suitors in fairy stories at answering conundrums in order to gain the hand of beautiful princesses. Problems therefore concern the choice of a best means towards an end.

We should not create too rigid a dichotomy between ends and means, because every end turns out to be a means towards another end. In addition, any given means may be infused by those values which convey, like a magnetic quality, the flavour of the ultimate end of all things and people. Consequently we cannot distinguish too closely between decision making and problem solving : what may appear to be a strategic judgement about ends turns out to be the problem of deciding upon the best of several courses in order to achieve the next higher level of aim or purpose. Thus one's mental frames of reference are constantly tilting and shifting, as if one were using navigating instruments at sea and not on secure land.

Alternatively, what seems to be a problem may therefore reveal the need for a decision, that the problem cannot be solved until we know what we want to do. As noted above, these end decisions become more abstract the higher up the continuum one moves, and therefore are both more deceptively simple and more challenging. Problems, as defined here, therefore focus attention upon the means rather than upon the choice of ends, although it may be reiterated that problems can – and frequently do – lead to a redefinition of objectives, aims or purposes.

Research into problem solving

The American psychologist A. Ruger carried out some of the earliest experiments in human problem solving. Published in 1910 in the *Archives of Psychology* (New York), his article describes the response of subjects to fairly simple mechanical puzzles, such as interlaced metal rings. Ruger noted that :

(i) most people tried to identify the significant area ('it must slip through this space') and the right order in time ('but first I must get it loosened here');

(ii) many found that the solution just happened, and they then analysed the process retrospectively ('How did I do it? I had the two pieces like this, then . . .');

(iii) finding the general or key principle comes first, and then the subject reconstructs the process step-by-step.

Karl Duncker, a German psychologist and pupil of Max Wertheimer, the founder of Gestalt psychology, set his subjects more complex tasks.[2] Like Ruger he made the subjects talk aloud during their attempts at problem solving. One celebrated example is the ray problem. Given a human being with an inoperable stomach tumour, and rays which destroy organic tissue at sufficient intensity, by what procedure can one free him from the tumour by these rays and at the same time avoid destroying the healthy tissue which surrounds it? Talking aloud, one subject groped his way towards a solution in the following manner :

send the rays through the oesophagus (the gullet);

desensitize the healthy tissues by chemical injections;

expose the tissue by operating.

[At this point the subject was given the reasons why all these possibilities were impractical.]

decrease the intensity of the rays so that they do not destroy healthy tissue and yet destroy the tumour;

swallow something opaque to the rays to protect the stomach walls;

alter the location of the tumour. . . . how? ;

introduce a drainage tube;

move the tissue towards the exterior;

vary the intensity of the rays;

adapt the healthy tissues by previous weak use of the rays;

somehow use diffuse rays . . . dispersed rays . . . stop . . .;

send broad and weak bundle of rays through a lens adjusted so that the tumour lies at the focal point;

send weak rays from different directions to converge on the tumour.

Duncker emphasizes the need to keep reformulating or restructuring the problem. The start of a new hypothesis is the rearrangement of all the factors which make up the problem situation. In the language of Chapter One, the subject tries out new syntheses of the given data. Duncker called it 'restructuration', or 'more precisely, this transformation of function within a system'. This led him to experiment with subjects in order to see how far they were able to perceive new functions for familiar objects.

Most solutions come about by the dialogue between previous experience and the present situation, or 'resonance' in Duncker's terminology. Success happens more or less by chance as the subject restructures (actually or mentally) the presented data, guided both by what he sees in the present and what he remembers from the past. Thus the problem solver may exhibit either the trial-and-error approach or a more analytical examination of the end (the goal) and means, before the 'resonance effects' provide the solution.

'Inspection may not have the last word, but at any rate it has the first,' he wrote. 'Its function is essentially heuristic', a searching for the decisive point of attack.[3] The preliminary stage includes analysis of the goal: 'what do I really want?' and perhaps the supplementary question, 'what can I do without?' According to Duncker, the heuristic method asks 'How shall I find the solution?', not 'How shall I attain the goal?' A solution is the way to a goal; a heuristic method, on the other hand, is the type of way to a solution.[4] Guided by heuristic methods the subject then reformulates the problem until 'the resonance effect of a signal' gives the solution.

Many of Duncker's problems are known today as 'functional fixedness' problems, and they all involve using a familiar object in a novel way. We tend to associate a particular object, person or word, with its customary function: the step of seeing a novel use may also be called dislocation of function. A hammer, for example, could serve as a doorknocker, bellclapper, or pendulum weight, instead of being used for driving in nails. The inhibition against novel use decreases with the lapse of time following normal use and the more time that passes since the object was used in its usual way the more likely you are to be a victim of functional fixedness.[5] There is some evidence that English schoolboys specializing in arts subjects are less prone to functional fixedness than science specialists.[6]

The easiest solution to a problem, declared Duncker, turns out to be, simply, if a then b. If one can reduce problems to these terms this will favour a speedy solution. Such a reduction happens when a has been so restructured that b can be read from it. Duncker also shows the value of having clues (or 'signals', as he called them). The more specific and definite they are the more they cut down the search for a solution. Models, signals, clues or hints – call them what you will – cut down the time spent in blind seeking or groping.

This latter aspect of Duncker's work has continued to interest both academics and practical managers. Take, for example, his word 'heuristics', which has appeared frequently in contemporary literature on problem solving, such as a *Harvard Business Review* article in October 1966 entitled 'Heuristic Programs for Decision Making'. What does it mean? Derived from the Greek and coined by 1860, 'heuristic' is defined in the *Shorter Oxford English Dictionary* as 'serving to find out; specifically applies to a system of education under which the pupil is trained to find out things for himself'. In current usage it has come to mean an operational maxim or rule of thumb for finding a solution. It serves as an umbrella term for more familiar concepts, such as rules of thumb, laws, strategies, policies, maxims and proverbs : i.e. general ways of going about things as opposed to specific clues or answers.

Duncker's long, difficult and often dull monograph *On Problem Solving* is far from clear either in structure or language, but its groping pioneer experiments and ideas have had a seminal influence. Several of his experiments are still used in management training today. Moreover, he has highlighted the distinction between 'organic' and 'mechanical' procedures, the former being the way it actually happens as the mind works in a new productive performance, while the latter is the shorter hindsight version. In teaching he suggests that the organic way of explanation should be followed, at the cost of the elegant brevity of the mechanical descriptions.

Phases of problem solving

There are hundreds of books and articles which attempt to outline the principle and techniques of problem solving. There is a wide measure of agreement on the main outline, which corresponds to the so-called 'scientific' method of investigation.[7]

BECOMING AWARE OF A PROBLEM AND DEFINING IT

General unease does not constitute a problem. There is something 'thrown forward' in one's path – a difficulty, obstruction or frustration – which has to be identified. Once known, the problem may be tackled or avoided, but until it has been defined it is not a problem as such.

SURVEYING THE DATA

Besides observation of the data this phase might also include an inspection of the materials involved or an exploration of the elements of the problem which have to be restructured. Sometimes the 'hidden factor', the key to the problem, will leap into significance at this stage, just as an important clue does to an alert detective. Mostly, however, the subject is busy analysing the components of the problem and their present structure as a synthetic whole.

ADVANCING HYPOTHESES

The synthesizing capacity of the mind is already at work, and now possible hypotheses for rearrangement or solution are suggested and elaborated. If none fit, the problem has to be analysed again, and possibly restated in terms of a fresh analysis of the goal and other hypotheses advanced.

MOVING TOWARDS A SOLUTION

Some partial solutions – getting sub-problems solved first – might be a necessary preliminary to a final assult on the problem. Emotion may accompany this phase – relief from tension, anger and disappointment, satisfaction or despair. The conclusions which stem from the chosen hypothesis are tested against known factors, or by experiment and the gathering of new facts, to see if they are valid and the hypothesis supported.

In the case of simple problems these stages may occur very quickly. Moreover, individual differences of approach, what could almost be called problem-solving styles, make themselves plain. These are not fixed, because people vary their approaches according to the nature of the problem. Yet there is a broad distinction, for example, between those who prefer the so-called 'analytical approach' (the slow step-by-step method of logical thinking), and those who tend to adopt the more indefinite and groping pattern of trial-and-error and the sudden intuitive restructuring of the whole problem that is characteristic of insight.

Background factors

The results of factual experiments in psychological laboratories have given us a general idea of what human beings do when confronted with a problem. Now we must look at the background factors or conditions which influence performance in problem-solving situations :

EXPERIENCE

This may be present in the problem solver's mind in varying degrees of specificity. At one end of the scale he may have encountered this precise problem before, and therefore know the solution at once. Secondly, he may have a general experience of this *genre* or family of problems. Thirdly, he may have some theories in his mind, and theories might be defined as abstract distillations of past experience. Writers on problem solving use a variety of words to describe this 'luggage' which the mind brings with it to a given problem, e.g. theory, model, set, direction and schema. All we can say is that problem-solving time is cut down when these relevant ideas are present.

Sometimes, however, the gap between these general ideas and the problem in hand is too wide, and some sort of clue or signal is necessary. Without such guidelines we can become entirely helpless when faced with a problem. The more specific and definite the clue the more likely we are to decode the problem into a solution.

Of course the ideas or ready-made constructs we bring with us may not fit the present situation. So deep is our need for some kind of theory, model or schema, that we too easily apply our past experience to the problem we perceive before us. Often the signals or clues which trigger off this mental reaction are the same as in a previous situation, and yet the repeated application of pre-conceived notions leads to the wrong solution. The mind's readiness to jump to conclusions by identifying a situation with others already experienced, through misreading accidental or deliberately false clues, leads to a large proportion of the errors in problem solving, as any detective story reader or writer knows. There is an optimum here between the past and the present : loyalty to past knowledge and experience balanced against an open and free-thinking capacity of being surprised by the uniqueness and never-before quality of the present.

MOTIVATION

Earlier in this book we noted the false dichotomy between thinking and feeling. The idea that effective problem solvers have to be cold calculating machines is far from the truth; as we have seen, emotion may accompany both the main intellectual activities of analysing, synthesizing and valuing, and also the phases or stages through which a decision maker or problem solver may move.

From the experimental evidence there seems to be an optimum for motivation in problem solving. Too much desire to solve a problem can impede one. High motivation can increase the tendency to persist in wrong or inappropriate directions. Too much emotional involvement is a handicap. This is one reason why boxers and wrestlers hope that their opponents will lose their tempers: over-anxiety, fury, tantrums, annoyance and intense distaste for the problem, all these can heighten the possibility that the subject will make mistakes. On the other hand, lack of interest, concern and involvement are equally a handicap. A certain degree of excitement and tension is necessary to get the best out of a person, and the human mind working at its best seems to have some sort of thermostat for maintaining the right motivational temperature.

At this point the significance of value-thinking comes out again. Values ought to give us a sense of proportion so that we rate or weigh the amount of emotion and time which we are prepared to devote to a given problem. The person with a sound sense of values and the capacity to use or apply them will tend to hit the right optimum on the motivational scales. Clearly this will depend upon the nature of the problem and the value of the solution.

CONCEPTS

The language or concepts used in problem solving are important. If one talks aloud while problem solving (as Duncker and Wertheimer suggest) or writes down the problem (as the British Army 'appreciation' method dictates) then there is a good chance that any unconsciously fixed idea or preconception will come to the surface. Often we are held up in problem solving because some pet assumption is blocking the way forwards (see page 84). As we shall see, one of the advantages of problem solving in groups is that others are more likely to challenge faulty premises or inappropriate concepts.

Conceptual thinking is closely linked with the useful but often misleading ability to categorize, or place things into classes. For example, the pencil that writes this sentence could be variously classified as tool, writing implement and finally pencil. Accepting the definition 'pencil' saves me a lot of time in responding to this particular long thin hard object : I know, for example, that it won't bite me. People like to have things, ideas and people in mental pigeon-holes according to concept, class or category : if they cannot do so they often show signs of anxiety.

Summary

For the leader, problems are essentially obstacles in the common path of himself and his team. His field of vision is as open as nature itself : it is not bounded by the artificial picture-frames of academic problems and questions. Yet he can learn from research into problem solving the need to sharpen his analytical faculties while retaining a flexibility in his powers of restructuring and synthesizing parts into new wholes. So far research has not thrown up any gold rules that can legitimately be transferred to the world of the manager, but it has enlarged our understanding and stimulated our imagination. Moreover, the steps or phases of problem solving (like those of decision making) provide a useful framework for training our mental faculties, particularly when the discipline involved has sunk deep into our depth minds.

CHAPTER SIX

CREATIVE THINKING

It is a major contention in this book that there is no sharp (or blunt) dichotomy between different types of thinking. In that aspect of thinking and doing called here synthesizing, the assembly of parts into a whole which is more than the sum of them, we have an elementary form of creation. In this respect we may say that the vast majority of people are creative. A little further up the scale or continuum we find the less common ability to combine or unite in an unexpected way apparently dissimilar parts for a given object. This capacity for invention or construction, contrivance or design, we might best call ingenuity.

We rightly reserve the extreme right of the continuum or scale for original productions of human intelligence or powers: for example, great scientific discoveries or works of art. It is the quality of outstanding originality – a value-judgement by universal consensus – which sets creativity at this level apart from other points on the scale of making, forming, producing or bringing into existence.

Creativity in any stretch of this continuum should not be confused with productivity, the bringing forth of goods in quantity. Sometimes quantity and quality go together, but this is not always so. One novelist may write two or three hundred novels and be forgotten; another may write one book which is truly original and which will live. It is not true, of course, that if a writer or inventor is exceptionally fertile or creative in the productivity sense, his work is necessarily inferior in creative quality: among playwrights, for example, the name of Shakespeare at once refutes the false but not uncommon inference that more means worse.

As we have seen, creative thinking at the level of synthesizing and resynthesizing (sometimes called restructuring) plays a part in both decision making and problem solving because it is one of the fundamental elements of deliberate thinking. Needless to say, ingenuity frequently comes into both processes as well. Occasionally highly original solutions or courses of action are thought up as well. But when we come to the higher reaches of the creativity continuum we see some significant differences, which are worth considering in a book primarily on decision making because of the light which they throw upon thinking in general, the raw material or stuff of all decisions.

We may explore the contrast by certain propositions which, if not always true, are generally so. In comparison to decision making, where the goal is either given or deducible from aims, the creative thinker (at this level) may accept or choose not to start from the stated or assumed objective. Creativity of a high order may throw up a whole new range of aims and objectives.

To the eyes of the predominantly decision-orientated manager the creative thinker may also show signs of what appears to be a lack of decisiveness. In his summary of research into the creative personality, after noting the persistence into maturity of childlike (but not childish) attributes such as a spirit of wonder, a capacity for rapture and a certain openness closely akin to gullibility, Dr Haefele noted that growth into adulthood brought the creative person, along with such fruits as confidence and sensitivity to oblique thoughts, 'deferment of judgement, and its other face, ability to see others' viewpoints; [which] may lead to apparent vacillation or indecision. This is partly true, but partly comes from insistence on keeping as many avenues of choice open as long as possible.'[1]

Therefore the creative thinker may have to free himself or herself from the goal-orientation which is necessary in other major shapes or patterns of thinking (and, incidentally, heavily rewarded socially and financially). In the 1930s the psychologist Marion Miller writing under the pseudonym 'Joanna Field' gave a valuable introspective account of her own depth mind at work, in which she described how she began to wonder whether :

... Life might be too complex a thing to be kept within the bounds of a single formulated purpose, whether it would not burst its way out, or if the purpose were too strong, perhaps grow distorted like an oak whose trunk had been encircled with an iron band.... (I began to guess that my self's need was for equilibrium, for sun, but not too much, for rain, but not always. I felt that it was as easily surfeited with one kind of experience as the body with one kind of food, and that it had a wisdom of its own, if only I could interpret it.) So I began to have an idea of my life, *not as the slow shaping of achievement to fit my preconceived purposes, but as the gradual discovery and growth of a purpose which I did not know.*[2]

Marion Miller contrasted her 'discovery' with the handbooks which told her to define the main purpose and the subordinate purposes. But introspection revealed that her mind was always wandering. It took time for her to accept this tendency 'but I had at least begun to guess that my greatest need might be to let go and be free from the drive after achievement – if only I dared. Then I might be free to become aware of some other purpose that was more fundamental ... something which grew out of the essence of one's own nature.'[3]

From this tentative conclusion there developed a different attitude to thought. 'It seemed as if I had been used to treating thought as a wayward child which must be bullied into sitting in one place and doing one thing continuously, against its natural inclination to go wandering, to pick one flower here and another there, to chase a butterfly or climb a tree. So progress in concentration had at first meant strengthening my bullying capacity.'[4] In other words, the mind could be set at 'wide focus' as well as narrow.

As a result Marion Miller had a sharpened awareness of the 'whole' in paintings, for example. This vision could be hindered by too much desire and expectancy. She found that emotion formed a dimension in thinking : 'Moods also had an absolute quality.' Happiness or despair presented themselves as absolutes, colouring the future as well as the present. Tiredness could allow a really unimportant worry to dominate her mind. The part played by feelings was much larger than she had supposed. This feeling-laden thinking which ignored or patronized the facts she called 'blind thinking'. She noted that 'blind thinking' desired extremes, either/or choice; it could swing with disconcerting suddenness, from superiority to inferiority, success to failure, present to past. Studying the facts could check this sudden tilting, especially the facts of time.

Not least, as others have confirmed, fear inhibits the wandering of thought. Marion Miller referred to 'those continually present fears which had so often prevented me from emerging into the fresh air of wide, purposeless attention.'[5] She knew the desire to hide a painful thought from oneself as much as from others, and the flood of panic impulses 'which tried to rush me to greater effort at the first hint of difficulty'. Anxiety could also stem from the unexamined values by which the self (or one's thinking) was judged : 'In face of the hard facts of my own imperfections, it set me all sorts of impossible standards without knowing it.'

Eventually Marion Miller struck upon the concept : 'Think backwards, not forwards.' The clue to thinking (or living, as she would put it) lay in the right relation between the surface and the depth minds. 'What I had to do, in the conscious phase of my thinking, was not to strain forward after new ideas, but deliberately to look back over the unconscious phase and see what bearing the ideas there thrown up had upon the matter in hand . . .'

From the above quotations it is clear that despite some fundamental links which show that by origins they belong to the same family or kind of thinking, creative or original thinking takes a markedly different shape to decision making or problem solving. In particular it cannot be classified as a sub-division or branch of the latter, although there are close or tenuous connections between them, depending on a given situation. Creative thinking can go on when there is no problem presented to the mind; as with aims and objectives it can throw up new problems and questions. On the other hand, the creative faculty of the depth mind can be harnessed to problem solving.

The study of creative thinking at the point of unusual originality confirms that in these cases there is frequently a flash of significance. This may be like a blinding flash of lightning or a tiny crackle as a spark leaps from one idea to another. Perhaps more often it is the sudden realization that two or more parts have been welded (in the unconscious mind) into a whole, plus the more-or-less instant *instinctive* judgement that the new combination is right. But there is an element of surprise and perhaps delight, although this may be foreshadowed by a sense of expectancy, a feeling of being on the right track. These experiences do not necessarily guarantee the originality of the creation; this depends upon a much wider judgement of its quality in the context of its concentric frames of reference.

Individuals clearly vary in their originality, and some psychologists have tried to distinguish the traits of the more creative thinkers. They come up with long lists of such qualities as intelligence, general knowledge, fluency, flexibility, originality, independence, scepticism, awareness, orientation to achievement, humour, psychological health, persistence, self-confidence, nonconformity, less-than-normal anxiety, dynamism and integration. Such lists share the same disadvantages as those listing the traits of leaders : they do not agree with each other and tell us little that is peculiar to creative people, for there are many people who have some of the above qualities but are not particularly original. To say that creative people have 'originality' does not get us very far.

There is agreement, however, that certain conditions favour original or inventive thought. From a careful reading of the C. S. Forester, Sir Lawrence Bragg and 'Joanna Field' quotations above, the diligent reader may note the following characteristics :

1. Thinking is allowed to play upon the materials at hand. The mind is set in wide focus, and thus it observes or takes in what others would eliminate as irrelevant or accidental. Goals or problems, although of interest, do not dominate the foreground of the mind. There is a willingness to scrap the present goal or problem altogether if something more interesting (within the overall purpose) crops up. Here the mind is like a hanging sticky paper with which ideas collide like flies.

2. Besides the present data the depth mind is well-stocked by background experience or reading in a variety of fields rather than any one speciality. As Pasteur wrote : 'Chance only favours invention for minds which are prepared for discoveries by patient study and persevering efforts.'

3. There are periods of conscious work when the relationships between the material is analysed as well as the question or problem being carefully formulated and perhaps reformulated several times.

4. There is a friendly and often humorous interest in the depth mind and its vagaries. This may be traced in the metaphors or images which writers use about it. R. L. Stevenson, for example, wrote about 'the little people ... my Brownies ... who do one-half my work for me while I am fast asleep, and in all human likelihood do the rest for me as well, when I am wide awake and fondly suppose I do it for myself'.

5. There is a definite organic or holistic dimension in their minds, revealed by the frequent use of the word growth and also a marked preference for organic metaphors and analogies. But this

holistic attitude (to life as well as thinking) is complemented by rigorous analytical skills and the ability to judge one's own work.

Inventions and scientific discovery

The first of the above characteristics can be swiftly illustrated by the many examples of famous inventions or discoveries hit upon by chance, from the days of Archimedes to our own :

In 1822, the Danish physicist Oersted, at the end of a lecture, chanced to put a wire conducting an electric current near a magnet, which eventually led to Faraday's invention of the electric dynamo.

In 1889, Professors von Mering and Minowski were operating on a dog when an assistant noticed a swarm of flies being attracted to the dog's urine. He mentioned it to Minowski, who found that the urine contained sugar. This was the first step towards the control of diabetes.

In 1929, Sir Alexander Fleming noticed that a culture of bacteria had been accidentally contaminated by a mould. This led to his discovery of penicillin.

This attribute of original creative thinking in itself creates some administrative problems. Managers and administrators tend to be goal-orientated in the sense discussed in Chapter Three. If they employ a scientist or creative man they usually want to define with him the goal of the research, the plan for it, the criteria of evaluation and so on. But a high proportion of original inventions will be accidents, unplanned fusions suddenly flashing into consciousness, while the alert mind is pursuing some other line, or perhaps working with no clear idea where it would lead. This fact has an important bearing on government and industrial policies in the provision of funds for various types of research, and particularly for research which seems to have no immediate practical application.

In a study prepared for the National Science Foundation of America, a group of scientists at the Illinois Institute of Technology made this point in a telling way by listing five important modern inventions which resulted from such 'pure research' :

'The video tape recorder was made possible by the development of magnetic recording techniques originally intended for sound recording alone, in combination with the principle of frequency modulation – which was patented in the United States as long ago as 1902. Electronic control theory, dating back to 1920, was also an important factor in the development of video tape. Thus, much

95

of the essential work had been done long before the first television station went on the air.

The contraceptive pill was a product of hormone research begun in the nineteenth century and later fertilized by the development of steroid chemistry. An important stage was the extraction of sapogenins – substances resembling cholesterol – from the Mexican wild yam. The oral contraceptive has wide biological implications which still remain to be investigated – so that it, in its turn, may produce unexpected yields of knowledge in other fields.

In the case of the electron microscope, there was a convergence of different streams of research on the wave nature of light and electrons, electron sources and optics. But it was a product developed for different purposes, the cathode ray tube, which supplied the high vacuum technology that made electron-microscopy feasible.

For non-scientists, the least familiar of the five inventions is probably matrix isolation, a technique for arresting and observing chemical reactions, which has wide uses in the study of high energy propellants, petroleum refining and synthetic materials. Many different lines of chemical and cyrogenic research contributed to the first definitive description of a matrix isolation procedure at the University of California in 1956. The future of space flight with solid fuels, cheaper petroleum refining and other essential technologies will depend on this discovery. Of all the research work which the scientists found to have contributed to the discovery of matrix isolation none was listed as devoted to the development of a particular product for a practical purpose defined in advance; yet the implications for the future of industrial chemistry now seem almost limitless.'[6]

The Illinois group came to the conclusion that in the case of the pill, videotape and the electron microscope, three-quarters of the research necessary had been completed before its practical application was understood and purposeful development was begun. In all five discoveries, the conscious development took place over quite a short period compared with the time it took for the essential pure research.

In a perceptive review of *The Double Helix*, the account by the scientist James Watson of how he and Francis Crick discovered the structure of DNA, Professor C. H. Waddington comments upon the difference of emphasis between decision making (with a goal in mind) and problem solving on the one hand, and the more characteristic method of scientific discovery on the other :

> Not only was the situation Watson describes, of a highly com-
> petitive race for a well-defined goal, rather unlike the condi-
> tions in which most science is done, but also the type of think-
> ing he used is not typical of most science. Watson approached
> DNA as though it were a super-complex jigsaw puzzle; a puzzle
> in three dimensions and with slightly flexible pieces.
>
> Solving a puzzle like that demands very high intelligence, and
> Watson gives a vivid blow-by-blow account of how he did it.
> But this is not the sort of operation that was involved in such
> major scientific advances as Darwin's theory of evolution,
> Einstein's relativity or Planck's quantum theory. And one is
> struck by how little Watson used a faculty which usually plays
> a large part in scientific discovery, namely intuitive understand-
> ing of the material.
>
> I will mention two examples, one more technical, one con-
> cerned with more abstract logic. When Watson was trying to
> fit together certain molecules, known as thymine and quanine,
> known to occur in two alternative forms, he just copied the
> shapes out of a chemical textbook and had not a trace of
> technical intuition as to which shape was more probable.
>
> Again, on the more abstract level, the whole of genetics is
> concerned with one thing turning into two, or occasionally two
> turning into one; the number three never comes into the picture.
> Yet Watson spent a lot of time trying to work out a three-
> stranded structure for DNA. The very idea of threes would
> make all one's biological intuition shudder. Of course, intuition
> can be drastically wrong; but it is usually a strong guide in
> innovative thinking.[7]

What *The Double Helix* does bring out, however, in a very
vivid way is how emotion accompanies the various phases of thinking, and how even in first-class scientific work competition can be
a stimulus to more general motivations.[8]

Despite the inevitable presence of mixed motives there is a strong
tradition in science attesting to the greater value of the relatively
purer or less self-infected forms of interest and curiosity. In the
greater creative minds this apparently simple or unmixed desire
can take on an attractive childlike quality. Einstein once told a
friend :

> When I asked myself how it happened that I in particular dis-

covered the Relativity Theory, it seemed to lie in the following circumstance. The normal adult never bothers his head about space-time problems. Everything there to be thought about, in his opinion, had already been done in early childhood. I, on the contrary, developed so slowly that I only began to wonder about space and time when I was already grown up. In consequence I probed deeper into the problem than an ordinary child would have done.[9]

The analogy with childhood and the attitude to work akin to a boy's love of playing appeared much earlier in a celebrated and profound remark attributed to Newton shortly before his death : 'I know not what I may appear to the world, but to myself I appear to have been only like a boy playing on the seashore, and diverting myself in now and then finding a smoother pebble or a prettier shell than ordinary, whilst the great ocean of truth lay all undiscovered before me.'[10]

Turning from scientific invention and discovery to art, the same characteristics of 'wide focus' attention and a willingness to abandon apparently fundamental preconceptions hold good. The British sculptor Reg Butler, for example, could declare in a lecture to art students :

> I have often myself recognized the fact that however exciting the ideas appear to be which I take to the studio in the morning, if I have not forgotten about them within half-an-hour, then that working day is a bad one. One of the first things one learns about being a working artist as opposed to a theoretician, is that the work comes from a level far below the top of one's head, and that, for all one knows, one's life is largely determined by the seemingly spontaneous behaviour of one's hands.[11]

Both the examples of C. S. Forester and Sir Lawrence Bragg illustrate the critical part played by preparation before any discovery or invention. The materials that will be broken down and fused together in new combinations in the depth mind can find their way to 'the bottom of the sea' only through the surface mind. Reading, talking to interesting people, visits and travel may all contribute to this end. Without the voyage of HMS *Beagle,* for example, Darwin might well have never 'discovered' the origin of the species. In a similar way experiences drawn from Somerset Maugham's travels coloured his stories and novels.

Yet there does seem to be an optimum, a 'not too little, not too much'. The avaricious reader, compulsive globe-trotter or party-goer does not seem to be among the more creative people. Indeed Einstein is said to have told his students not to read too many books. Certainly the shape or formulation of other people's ideas can play tricks with the development of one's own thoughts. C. S. Forester clearly preferred fact-filled manuals, the dry tinder upon which the creative spark could fall. One might perhaps distinguish between these larder-stocking readings and experiences, and the few paragraphs, incidents or personal encounters – supercharged with interest or emotion – which find their way still struggling and alive to the lowest fathoms of the depth mind.

In this context we should note the importance of the creative thinker finding his appropriate field. There are few people who show outstanding originality or discovery in more than one field. Besides being a sphere which engages their interest and curiosity at a deep level, it must lend itself to their particular imaginative abilities. We might group the main types of these as follows, stressing that although they are not mutually exclusive one tends to predominate over the others in any one person. They are all concerned with patterns or relationships :

VERBAL : easily perceived relationships between words; concepts or ideas which can be verbalized in the chosen medium; good memory for written or spoken words. (Writers, poets, sociologists, philosophers, theologians, etc.)

SPATIAL : spatial relationships easily perceived; imaginative ability to think in three dimensions; can remember spatial arrangements. (Artists, architects, some scientists, town planners, engineers.)

NUMERATE : relationships between figures easily perceived; capable of working out complex mathematical calculations mentally; good memory for numbers. (Pure mathematicians, some scientists, etc.)

COLOUR : relationships between colours easily perceived; colour schemes can be swiftly visualized; good memory for colours. (Artists, dress designers, interior decorators, etc.)

MUSICAL : relationships between sounds easily perceived; music can be composed mentally; good memory for tunes. (Composers, singers, jazz musicians, etc.)

99

In the case of genius the memory can become 'photographic' in any of the above aspects: Mozart, for instance, could remember precisely every piece of music he ever heard. But this sort of photographic memory does not guarantee genius (as quiz winners demonstrate); it is only one card in the winning hand the genius holds and in isolation has relatively little value.

Consequently the problem solver and above all the creative thinker must find the right *milieu* for their particular intellectual talents, like a wrestler who cannot demonstrate his individual skill to the full unless he is matched with an opponent whose style allows him to do so.

Lastly, the literature on scientific discovery and creative thinking bears out the close relation between thinking and feeling. Emotions precede, accompany and crown creative achievement. It may be that a well-balanced emotional life and a sensitive awareness of the movements of feelings 'too deep for words' are pre-conditions for effective creative or inventive thinking. Be that as it may, the outstanding thinker in any field is paid in the coinage of joy: a sudden overflow of excited feelings or a more lasting and quieter sense of profound fulfilment. After demonstrating the feasibility of protecting people against smallpox by vaccination, Edward Jenner wrote: 'The joy I felt at the prospect before me of being the instrument destined to take away from the world one of its greatest calamities ... was so excessive that I sometimes found myself in a kind of reverie.'

CHAPTER SEVEN

DECISIONS ABOUT PEOPLE

Learning is not wisdom; information does not
guarantee good judgement.
JOHN DEWEY

'Selection of top management is probably the most important of
all decisions – for example, about board membership. A is retiring,
in four years' time : B and C follow soon after. Who are the
likely candidates? There is now time to position them so that
experience will equip them for the board.' These comments by
Dr Ernest Woodroofe, Chairman of Unilever, would meet with
wide agreement among the most senior managers in industry and
top leaders in other spheres. Next to major policy decisions, the
most important decisions facing managers are those about people.[1]

This simple fact would not be deducible from the majority of
recent books and articles with decision making or decisions in
their titles. On the contrary, the prevalent opinion among their
writers seems to be that mathematical or algebraic decisions are
all-important. The assumption seems to be, as one manager put
it : 'What cannot be quantified is not worth considering.' Doubt-
less mathematical models and computers are valuable tools for
decision makers in large organizations, but they are much less
useful in the decisions that senior managers regard as really
important : major policy directions and decisions about people.

Nor is that other *genre* of management literature, books on
interviewing methods and techniques, much help at this point.
Apart from offering some often sound advice on the conduct of
interviews, these books usually exhort the manager to analyse the
job and the candidate as thoroughly as possible. The principle is
square pegs for square holes.

Attempts are frequently made to define what is required in the manager's personality; to work out a list or pattern of traits which become the theory or schemata in the interviewer's mind. So far no agreement has been reached upon what the qualities of an ideal manager are, and it is to be doubted whether they will ever be defined to everyone's satisfaction. Qualities of leadership are as subject to fashion as ladies' hats and men's ties.[2]

This is not to say, however, that the analyst of personality has no part to play in the selection of people. But analysis is only one of the three basic forms of thinking; it is a pretender to the throne who should be kept firmly down by the other two members of the triumvirate. The application of scientific principles or the logical approach to decisions about people can never yield that kind of certainty which some text-books promise. In the last resort all our decisions about people are a form of judgement in the Webster's Dictionary definition of the latter word as 'a decision or conclusion on the basis of indications and probability when the facts are not clearly ascertained'. The aim of this chapter is to explore the nature of such judgements, and its argument is that all the dimensions of thinking described in Chapter One come into play when we make up our minds about people.

The analytical (mainly conscious) part of this process is too familiar to need much description. In terms of choosing people for job or role, the central concern here, as objective an analysis of the job or role in question as possible is clearly desirable, and through such techniques as job specification (which stemmed from work study) management is growing ever more competent in this aspect.

Opinions differ about the value of the analysis of the personality, temperament and aptitudes of people by written psychological tests and so-called depth interviews. It is perhaps a noticeable feature of senior and experienced managers, however, that they tend to take what could be called a more holistic approach. In other words they are more interested in the man's curriculum vitae, the growth story of his life, or what he has actually *done* in his life history so far. As people are entities who are more than the sum of their parts, holistic thinking is the most appropriate basis for judgement.

In contrast to the theorists (who are only gradually catching up on this point) the experienced senior leader, who is a proven good judge of men, is inclined to look at wholes much more often.

His synthesizing mind sees the man in relation to the organizational setting: a part who will change and be changed by the new working environment of the job in question. And so a man technically competent might be turned down for a job because he would not fit in, or because he would put people's backs up. Obviously if stressed too much this strand in judgement could lead to the stultifying conformity conjured up by William Whyte in *The Organization Man*, but within limits it enters into the total work of judgement.[3]

Mr Babington Smith of the Institute of Experimental Psychology at Oxford University has described a useful exercise to illustrate how our knowledge of a group or an individual 'grows' in a holistic way:

> The systematic observation of the activities of a group covers what is more easily evident in the observation of a single individual, 'getting to know' people. Information about a person accumulates, and the question is how best to record, process or employ it. The concept of 'unities' growing in extent and comprehensiveness may be useful here too. A model of 'getting to know' people may be demonstrated in the following way. Draw in turn, as numbered, the lines of the accompanying diagram and as each is drawn look at what is drawn and write briefly what is there.

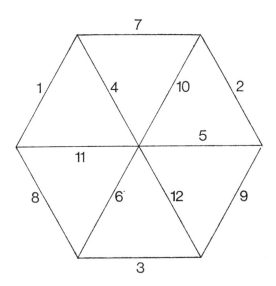

Most people find that at certain stages they see some well-known shape developing, and succeeding lines confirm and support this; but there are stages when they are taken aback by the next addition, and find that the earlier pattern has to be replaced by a new one. (This demonstration will undoubtedly lose by being presented in this way, where the end state can be seen; even so, it may be worth going through the steps or trying it on someone who does not know the final appearance.)

The implication of this model is that we 'get to know' people as 'wholes'. But for some people is seems to make sense to think of others in terms of assessable traits. Theories of personality devised by psychologists may be quite inappropriate for everyday use; it is highly relevant therefore to inquire how people are in fact found to observe and think about others, and inquiry based on the view that traits would be attributed to others on the basis of accumulating and enumerable instances has not borne it out. There is plenty of room for more exploration by observation of the ways in which people do get to know each other.[4]

It is interesting also that senior leaders tend to stress the importance of integrity in their judgements of people. In the many seminars with leaders of all levels and in the whole range of occupations at which I observed this fact, I have often asked those who introduced the word to define integrity but they rarely can to their own satisfaction. Lord Slim could define it only by its effects: 'The quality which makes people trust you.' Perhaps the reason for this vagueness is that the word describes something that by its nature is not susceptible to analysis: it is the synthetic or holistic term for 'wholeness' in human character. Sometimes definitions are offered which reduce it to honesty or being true to oneself ('Which self?' asked one college principal pertinently). Yet the *Shorter Oxford English Dictionary* defines it primarily as 'the condition of having no part or element wanting; unbroken state; material wholeness, completeness, entirety'.

The word integrity has significantly taken on a value dimension as well, for the same dictionary further defines it as 'soundness of moral principle; the character of uncorrupted virtue; uprightness, honesty, sincerity'. Whether we are consciously aware of it or not we are assessing the values and attitudes of the person we are making a decision about, and matching them against our own.

It helps to be aware of this fact. Coherence of values and attitudes is particularly important, if not vital, where trust is necessary in the working relationship. Trustworthiness rests largely on the foundations of moral values, especially if the relationship is to be exposed to testing situations. Then it helps if one knows that despite the inevitable and welcome differences between people there is a solid bedrock of agreement on fundamentals. As General de Gaulle said of Winston Churchill: 'We navigated by the same stars.'

In decisions about people the analysing, synthesizing and valuing attributes or facets of applied thinking are therefore hard at work, but there is a direction to them: they are seeking to predict what the person will do or be like in future situations. For example, if A tells jokes on three or four occasions, you may conclude he has a 'sense of humour', i.e. that in the future he is likely to go on making you laugh. You have observed in his past and present a pattern which leads in a certain direction towards the unknown future. Or if B lets you down on two or three occasions you may assess him as unreliable: you doubt whether he can be relied upon to stand by you when the going gets hard in the future.

Of course it is notoriously difficult to be certain about such predictions. There is a tendency to generalize from too few incidents or data. We may unconsciously have projected our own feelings, so that (on the same evidence) three judges may call one man stubborn, obstinate, or pig-headed. What seems bold to one, may be rash to another. Experience, which means evaluating the result of predictions made at a given point, can refine such judgements considerably, but possibly only within certain limits of natural ability.

Natural ability plus much experience can lead some people to become increasingly confident of that other notoriously gullible guide, first impressions. As one manger put it to me, 'Often I have changed my mind about a man but in the long run I usually return to my first impressions and find them well-founded.' The danger is that we give someone an imaginary halo or pair of horns on first meeting and then use all the subsequent evidence to confirm our first erroneous impression.

Where first impressions, measured by some objective or impartial standards, consistently prove to be correct the person concerned is considered to be intuitive, in the sense of swift or instant recognition of the nature of something or someone. Such people are consciously or unconsciously aware of small details – a glance, a gesture, the choice of a word – and perhaps at depth mind level match this information sifted against countless other patterns or constructs.[5] By first impressions is meant not necessarily first sight but the first sight, conversation and the initial two or three meetings. Such intuitive people learn a great deal about someone in the early hours of their relationship; later they may go on discovering more and more, but they are rarely in for major surprises : their sketch map of the person in predictive terms turns out to be fairly accurate.

Professor H. J. Eysenck mentioned such people in his lecture to the Institute of Personnel Management's 1970 National Conference : 'The vast majority of people are convinced they are good at judging others and in some there does seem to be a persistent personality trait which governs their ability to judge people in general. At present interviewers are not selected for their ability – their intuitive sensitivity to others – but this could be done.' Professor Eysenck expressed his belief that training for interviewers could be much improved, yet he emphasized the importance of selection. 'The reason why people make bad interviewers is that they increase the spread of their judgement too far. Many people are incapable of assimilating the complex character of another's personality and tend to over simplify,' he warned.[6]

'I have but a woman's reason, I think him so because I think him so,' quoth one of Shakespeare's ladies. But intuition is not restricted to women (although possibly their more holistic nature favours them), nor is it quite as arbitrary as that. It is based upon evidence which is assessed, however, with computer-like speed. Given sufficient significant data (which takes time) such intuition can become well-nigh infallible. The prediction by Jesus of Nazareth that Peter would deny him in the hours before the crucifixion illustrates this point, and incidentally serves also to keep such particular predictions within the framework of the overall decision about someone : 'You are Peter, and on this rock I will build my church.'

Many but by no means all leaders have possessed good judgement about people, which we might call educated intuition. The speed and ways in which the analysing, synthesizing and valuing functions of thought bombard like atoms our impressions both consciously and unconsciously will differ from individual to individual. Those who are outstandingly successful at it seem to have the right attitude of confidence mingled with suspicion towards their first impressions, a marked interest in the history involved, and competence in analysing, synthesizing and valuing at all levels of the mind. Despite a faith in what might be called an enlarged version of first impressions they distrust snap judgements, and prefer if possible to give their depth minds room to share in the decision. Judgements about people are said to ripen, an activity of the depth mind. Peter Drucker observed the same phenomena among effective executives : 'Without exception, they make personnel decisions slowly and they make them several times before they really commit themselves.'[7]

These intuitive powers, reinforced by much experience of life, can give the same people a surprising ability of unerring prediction in cases where the more purblind remain in the dark, a most useful ability in a leader at the higher levels. In the English Civil War, for example, General Sir William Waller, commanding an army in the West Country in the spring of 1645, observed with some amazement this faculty in a middle-aged but junior cavalry general temporarily attached to serve under him. It was the first time Waller realized that this officer possessed more than ordinary gifts. His name was Oliver Cromwell. Of him Waller wrote :

> As an officer he was obedient, and did never dispute my orders nor argue upon them. He did, indeed, seeme to have great cunning, and whilst he was cautious of his own words, not putting forth too many lest they should betray his thoughts, he made others talk, untill he had as it were sifted them, and known their inmost designs. A notable instances was his discovering in one short conversation with one Captain Giles ... that although his words were full of zeal, and his actions seemingly brave, that his heart was not with the cause : and in fine this man did shortly after join the enemy at Oxford, with three and twenty stout fellows.[8]

In conclusion, we know little or nothing about the ways in which managers actually make decisions about people, but we can assert that the primary colours of analysing, synthesizing and valuing are involved in various combinations. We can posit also with reasonable confidence that feelings and emotions may well colour thought and that it is important to be aware of how far they are being allowed to do so. Lastly, the holistic nature of such judgements, being both concerned with living and growing entities on the one hand and arising often from a time of gestation in the depth mind on the other, seems worthy of notice. It is in an area which merits much more research in the next decade.

CHAPTER EIGHT

EXPERIMENTS IN TRAINING

The object of this chapter is to review some of the more organized attempts at developing problem solving, decision making and creative thinking abilities in adults. The courses are arranged, as far as possible, in chronological order. I have treated each course under four headings: History, Content, Methods of Training and Evaluation. A short list of books on each course will be found at the back, in the 'Notes and Bibliography' for this chapter.

Synectics

HISTORY

'Synectics', a neologism, is defined by William J. J. Gordon in his book by that title as 'the joining together of different and apparently irrelevant elements'.[1] The original Synectics Group came together in Cambridge, Massachusetts, in 1944 to carry out research into the creative process by studying itself at work. In 1961 that group was still in existence, but had trained others in Arthur D. Little, Inc. (1952), Kimberley-Clark, Singer Sewing Machine Co., Johns-Manville, and RCA-Whirlpool.

CONTENT

William Gordon's account of the content of Synectics courses is somewhat confused. Fundamentally it consists of a study of the creative process gained from reading biographies and books on invention, a description of the necessary states of mind, and an expanded analysis of operational mechanisms, the so-called concrete psychological factors which are held to be capable of inducing or sustaining the desired mental habits or states attendant upon the production of technological novelty. Confusion comes from their inter-mixture in the text.

Synectics theory is best understood by outlining its historical development, a holistic approach which occupies much of Mr Gordon's book. In 1944 the founders observed and analysed one inventor's thought processes into the following states of mind: detachment-involvement; deferment (of premature solutions); speculation (letting the mind run free); autonomy of object (one solution coming alive). The rest of synectics theory both elaborated these states and suggested certain operational mechanisms which galvanize the mind into productivity.

In the latter context William Gordon and his associates emphasize the concepts of 'making the strange familiar' and then 'making the familiar strange'. They seem to regard the former as the straightforward preliminary analysis of the problem. They emphasize in particular the importance of making the familiar strange. Operational mechanisms necessary to get the mind into this particular orbit boil down to the liberal use of analogy and metaphor before attempting to make a new synthesis (as opposed to *ex post facto* explanative or decorative metaphors). Analogies are classified into personal ('How would I feel if I was this wind-screen wiper?'); direct (actual comparison of parallel facts, knowledge or technology); symbolic (objective impersonal images, as in poetry); and fantasy (more imaginative and further removed from reality). In particular the value of direct analogies with organic life and growth, in one form or another, is stressed and illustrated with some telling examples.

Besides these concrete psychological gambits the synectors advise us to be aware of, tolerate and make use of irrelevance. Their advice could be summed up as 'Cast about you and observe the apparently irrelevant'. The irrelevant is divided into three categories: perceptions, ideas and generalities; accidents (defined neatly as 'the irrelevant in motion'); and emotional factors. The latter include the 'hedonic response', the pleasurable feeling of being on the right track, closely connected to the perception of elegance and the 'autonomy of the object', or the sense that one solution is coming 'alive' of its own accord, like a baby being born. The hedonic response can be used by those who are aware of its existence as a kind of early warning system that a solution is on the way: it acts then as a filter of irrelevance. Lastly, there is the single criterion of 'does it work?'

In commenting upon the emotional factors present in groups (and presumably in individuals as well) the synectors also emphasized the importance of a strong sense of purpose. 'There is a direct relation between the strength and vitality of purpose ...and the soundness and novelty of the solution achieved in a given session'.[2] Of course it is industrial purposes which create the problems that the synectors were asked to solve, but the sessions themselves also have a creative purposefulness of their own, which William Gordon described thus : 'There appears to be a goal towards which the entire process tends; in fact, the whole unconscious purposefulness of a session is embodied in the state of autonomy of object. Although this state is operating all along, it is not clearly manifest until a solution begins to form. Then in retrospect, all the preceding effort appears purposeful and somehow directed.'

METHODS OF TRAINING

The group features prominently in the synectics movement, in the belief that 'a synectic group can compress into a few hours the kind of semi-conscious mental activity which might take months of incubation for a single person' (p. 10). In the off-shoots from the original Cambridge group much care was taken to select synectors on the following criteria : representation (of a company activity, e.g. finance, production); energy level (high, but not excessively so); age (over 25 and under 40); administrative potential (good generalizers); entrepreneurial talent; job background (diversity of experience much valued); education (a record for having shifted fields of major interest); and 'the "almost" individual' (one with general but unrealized potential). Nine other criteria are advanced for the final selection interview.

Training consisted of one week a month for twelve months. Reading, listening to tapes, explanation of the 'mechanisms', the citing of examples, practice on actual problems, widening of general knowledge, and the setting of group working standards occupy these weeks.

EVALUATION

Much of what we know about the creative process of problem solving is present in the content of synectic theory, but the relations between analysis and synthesis, the conscious and unconscious mind, operational mechanisms and states of mind are left too vague or implicit, despite an attempt in an apprendix to arrange it all into nine phases. Yet these American researchers had picked up some main lines : the part played by imagery in a working dialogue between surface and depth minds, the importance of growth or organic concepts – the holistic proclivity of the depth mind to see, respond and use stories or images of growth.

William Gordon's book gives us insufficient evidence about the training and educational methods employed to justify his claim that synectics theory had proved it possible to train at least certain people in creativity. Obviously the emphasis of this approach falls on selecting those with creative potential in the technological field. Also, length of time assigned to training restricts the applicability of synectics to a few rich companies. Yet it is quite possible that the same results would be achieved at less cost by involving more people and giving them a simple yet durable form of training. None the less synectics research has made a valuable contribution to our knowledge. The next method to be discussed – 'brainstorming' – has sought to evade these limitations.

Brainstorming

HISTORY

Perhaps the most widely known approach to producing ideas is the so-called 'brainstorming' method. The origins of this method go back to Alexander Osborn, whose book *Applied Imagination* first appeared in 1953, and has served as a primary textbook for 'brainstormers' ever since.[3] According to this book the first 'brainstorming' sessions were held in America in 1939. Alexander Osborn was a founder member of a large advertising company. His other books mainly extol 'creativity' as the key to success and happiness, and have little of training value in them.

CONTENT

The simple technique of brainstorming is to allow ideas to flow freely from a group without criticisms being voiced. The rules as laid down by Osborn[4] have not varied substantially since 1939.

Judicial judgement is ruled out. Criticism of ideas must be withheld until later. 'Free-wheeling' is welcomed. The wilder the idea, the better; it is easier to tame down than to think up. Quantity is wanted. The greater the number of ideas, the more the likelihood of winners. Combination and improvement are sought. In addition to contributing ideas of their own, participants should suggest how ideas of others can be turned into better ideas; or how two or more ideas can be joined into still another idea. The only strictly formal procedure laid down is that there should be a written record of the ideas produced.

METHODS OF TRAINING

Twenty to thirty minutes is probably about the limit for a brain-storming session on a particular subject, but changes of topic allow several almost consecutive sessions. A normal seminar of one day's length on brainstorming includes some practice sessions and an explanation of how various barriers and constraints can limit our thinking. For example, the course members at a British Institute of Management day in 1969 were encouraged to consider the uses to which a leather belt could be put and to reject assumed constraints, such as not chopping it up.

This fundamental method is capable of much variation. For example, in the 'waste-not' method the group is shown an apparently valueless by-product or waste factory item, and is asked to brainstorm uses. In the 'and-also' method a suggestion is made and taken up by every member of the group with contributions which each amount to 'Yes, and also this would make it even more effective.' The 'tear-down' method's object is to think of all the limitations, failings or drawbacks of a specific product. Afterwards they can be studied for possible remedies.

Training of group leaders in these methods is important. As Osborne pointed out, 'fiascos are usually due to failure of leader-ship.'[5]

EVALUATION

The more common criticisms of brainstorming fall into two categories: first, that it frequently does not rest upon adequate problem definition and secondly, that no attention is given to evaluating or testing the ideas thrown up by group discussion to see whether or not they work. In other words, if practised in isolation, the technique leaves out the analysing and valuing themes of the thinking altogether. Hence the tendency to in-corporate brainstorming into a fuller process of decision making or problem solving, whether undertaken by a group (as in synectics) or by the individual who convenes (and possibly leads) a brainstorming session.

Certainly, with regard to the first criticism, brainstorming works best on specific and limited but open-ended problems. Given these criteria and the valuable suspension of judgement it is a technique for stimulating a quantity of ideas. Products and advertisements lend themselves to brainstorming. For original creative work, which requires extensive preparatory work, depth mind activity and the guidance-system of values, it is much less effective. It is positively harmful as a philosophy: namely that 'group-think' can replace individual creativity.

There are relatively few objective research articles on brainstorming. According to one study the quantity and quality of solutions increased in brainstorming groups as compared to those which also allowed critical evaluation of ideas. Yet another researcher found that both kinds of groups produced ideas of the highest quality: brainstormers merely threw up more low quality ideas. Originality did not come into the definition of 'quality' in these two articles.[6]

A more important study compared individual as opposed to group brainstorming, and offered the conclusions that although a group can produce more ideas than one individual, a number of individuals working alone can throw up more ideas than the same number working as a group. Moreover, the individuals working on their own produce ideas of a higher average quality.[7] Dr Haefele concluded: 'A person alone is still freer in thought that one in a brainstorming group, despite the suspend-judgement, no-criticism rule.'[8]

Clearly one issue in the debate is how far does quantity in itself lead to right choices? Perhaps a brainstorming group can be compared to a computer which can produce many more possibilities for moves than chessmasters, but lacks the human ability to single out without extensive analysis the most likely possible move.[9]

The evaluation evidence from laboratory tests is inconclusive. Certainly we can say that brainstorming stimulates a free flow of ideas, but thereafter the group dimension may become less important. In other words group brainstorming may be a good way of teaching creative thinking to individuals who may later work characteristically on their own or in loose associations, such as laboratories. With regard to the latter respect, in some ways brainstorming is an artificial simulation of what occurs naturally in any community. It usually takes several sticks to light a fire. Research continues into the effects of creative problem-solving courses based on brainstorming held at the University of Buffalo and other educational institutions in America, including some schools.[10]

Dr Abercrombie

HISTORY

In 1960 M. L. Johnson Abercrombie's book *The Anatomy of Judgement* was published, containing the results of ten years of research into the problems of teaching medical students to be scientific or objective, or 'in more precise terms, to obtain information of good predictive value from a given situation'.[11] As a teacher of zoology, Dr Abercrombie had been disappointed with the effects that learning about science seemed to have on habits of thinking, especially upon the ability of students to use scientific ways of thinking to solve problems presented in a slightly new way. After 1945 Dr Abercrombie worked in the Department of Anatomy at University College, London, and (with financial support from the Rockefeller Foundation) evolved an eight session course in thinking for medical students.

The preparation for the course involved some creative thinking from Dr Abercrombie, for she brought together parts drawn from such apparently diverse fields as group analytical psychology and research on visual perception.

What is judgement? 'Our reaction to the present bombardment of information involves ignoring some of it, seizing the rest and interpreting it in the light of past experience in order to make as good a guess as possible about what is going to happen. This may be called a process of judgement; that is, making a "decision or conclusion on the basis of indications and probabilities when the facts are not clearly ascertained" (Webster 1934). We are continually selecting from the information presented, interpreting it with information received from the past, and making predictions about the future.'[12]

CONTENT

Each of the eight sessions lasted about ninety minutes. The first three sessions dealt with seeing, the fourth with language, the next with classification, the sixth with the evaluation of evidence, the seventh with causation and the last session reviewed the course.

The message of the whole course was summed up by Dr Abercrombie on the last page of her book :

In receiving information from a given stimulus pattern we select from the total amount of information available (that is, from the complex of the stimulus pattern in its context) and from our own store of information. The receipt of information therefore involves making a judgement, but in many cases (as for instance in seeing familiar things) this is done so rapidly and automatically that we are unaware of the extent of our personal involvement in the act, tending to regard the information as given. In such cases we might obtain more valid information if we could consider alternative selections from the information available.

Many factors of which we are unconscious influence our judgements, both in cases where we are not aware of making any (as in seeing) and in those where we are (as in evaluating evidence from an experiment). It is postulated that we might make more valid judgements if we could become conscious of some of these factors. A situation (free group discussion) is described in which alternative judgements of the same stimulus pattern are discussed, and some of the factors influencing the judgements become apparent. The validity of the contribution of the various factors can then be assessed. The results of a test support the hypothesis that judgement is improved after this experience.'[13]

Boiling this down a little further we could say that Dr Abercrombie urges us to analyse the evidence in front of us, particularly in relation to its context (the parts-and-the-whole); and, secondly, in relation to our schemata (as she called them) – the general concepts from various sources stored in our conscious or unconscious minds, which we bring with us to our mental work. All this to the end that we should have more possibilities of choice open to us. Owing to the tricks and vagaries of our perception and our tendency to impose patterns or read meanings which are not there, we have a bias towards limiting prematurely the possibilities, courses of action or interpretations open to us.

METHODS OF TRAINING

The experiments were conducted under the wing of a university department of Anatomy and it is hardly surprising that Dr Abercrombie adopted methods which would be familiar to her students. Instead of giving eight lectures she presented the students individually with an exercise (e.g. to compare and interpret two radiographs), which served as the basis for a group discussion. The exercise involved the student in writing down his reactions to a given stimulus.

Dr Abercrombie laid much stress upon what she called 'free group discussion', the central characteristic of this method being that the students talk more among themselves than to the teacher, who becomes mainly a listener and a guide. The emphasis in the course upon awareness led Dr Abercrombie to experiment with group discussion as the means by which we can become (through the comments of others) conscious of what previously was unconscious. 'Discussion in a group does for thinking what on real objects does for seeing,' she wrote. 'We become *aware* of discrepancies between different people's interpretations of the same stimulus, and are driven to weigh the evidence in favour of alternative interpretations.'[14]

EVALUATION

In the last three years of the experiment half the total class of medical students took the course in the first term, and the other half during the second term. At the end of the first term they all sat a test in observation and reasoning, and in comparison with the control group the taught students different in the following respects. The taught students made more descriptive statements and fewer inferences, and they tended more than the others to give the evidence for their inferences. Although they did not make significantly more true inferences (which required anatomical knowledge they lacked at this stage, or luck) fewer among the taught made false inferences, which suggests that they had become more critical of evidence. In answer to a question about the position of a humerus (arm bone) in two radiographs, three times as many students in the taught half explicitly referred to two inferences than in the control group. By juxtaposition of apparently similar tests it was possible to find out how far the students approached each problem as a new one, instead of blindly applying the solution to an old one. The numbers of taught students showing a fixed attitude in this way was smaller than among the control group.

The most common favourable reaction by students to the course was that it made them think. In many cases it had a delayed effect: only several months later – in one instance, two years – did some course members claim to have understood it. There were useful by-products: expression and comprehension, public speaking and the skill of listening.

'It seems likely that the changes were of a generalized kind', concluded Dr Abercrombie, 'and would affect other kinds of behaviour, for example, reasoning from experimental results, but we were not able to investigate them.'[15]

Dr Abercrombie noted that discussion techniques were used 'here and there in industry and commerce in ways more and less sophisticated, to stimulate problem solving activities and "creative" or "productive" thinking'. But she thought the methods described in her book, suitably adapted, could be most useful in the teaching of children. Certainly academic work lends itself readily to her approach and methods; for example, I found them extremely valuable in the context of teaching historical thinking to 18–21 years old students at Sandhurst. There is no reason to doubt that the same approach and methods could have an important contribution to make to the teaching of history (and all subjects, for that matter) in schools. Yet they also have a vital part in management education.

Kepner and Tregoe

HISTORY

Charles H. Kepner (social psychologist) and Benjamin B. Tregoe (sociologist), joint authors of *The Rational Manager: A Systematic Approach to Problem Solving and Decision Making* (1965), met in the 1950s while working for the RAND Corporation in California on advanced systems of defence for the US Airforce.[16] In their own time they studied the effects of automation in industry and by this route came eventually to decision making. Finding little help in the literature they decided to study actual case-studies of problem solving in industry. It took them five years to evolve their own process of problem analysis (1959–64). Using patented materials the authors have engaged in management training in problem solving and decision making on both sides of the Atlantic. Apparently, in 1968, when the Apollo space capsule blew up killing three astronauts, Dr Kepner and Dr Tregoe were called in to discover the cause. Since 1965 some five thousand British managers have been through the Kepner-Tregoe mill. The training has also spread to the Far East, South Africa and South America.

CONTENT

The Kepner-Tregoe approach is based on their definition of a problem as a deviation from a standard, and a cause as an unplanned, unexpected change. 'Failures in problem solving trace back to one basic fact: a problem cannot be solved unless its cause is known. A problem is an unwanted effect, something to be corrected or removed. It was brought about by some specific event or combination of events. To get rid of the effects efficiently you must know how it came to be. Any decision based on a false cause is going to be ineffective, wastefully expensive and sometimes downright dangerous. Here it should be noted that every problem has only one real cause. It may be a *combination* of events and conditions operating as if they constituted a single event.'[17]

The process therefore consists of defining the problem by contrasting what should be happening with the actual phenomena, finding the cause of the deviational change, and then making a sound decision about it by choosing from the available possibilities the best one.

This approach lays heavy emphasis on identifying precisely the cause of the deviation from a standard, and to that end recommends certain principles. 'The problem analyst has an expected standard of performance, a "should" against which to compare actual performance. A problem is a deviation from a standard of performance. A deviation from standard must be precisely identified, located and described. There is always something distinguishing that which has been affected by the cause from that which has not. The cause of a problem is always a change that has taken place through some distinctive feature, mechanism, or condition to produce a new, unwanted effect. The possible causes of a deviation are deduced from the relevant changes found in analysing the problem. The most likely cause of a deviation is one that exactly explains all the facts in the specification of the problem'.[18]

The process for covering these steps is further analysed into fourteen basic concepts, seven each on problem solving and decision making. Problem solving is held to be the necessary preliminary activity before decision making.

Since 1965 the Kepner-Tregoe course has expanded to include : Situational Analysis, which entails determining the priority area of concern and choosing one of the three methods of analysis below which is most appropriate to it; Problem Analysis, i.e. finding the cause of a problem (as above); Decision Analysis, which means choosing the best course of action; and Potential Problem Analysis, which ensures the successful implementation of a decision by analysing possible problems.

METHODS OF TRAINING

Training programmes based on the fourteen concepts have been developed for senior and middle managers (the APEX course); for middle junior managers and supervisors (the GENCO course); for sales/managers and supervisors (the VERTEX course), and for government departments and non-profit making organizations (the FBA course). Kepner-Tregoe also train and license managers as course leaders to carry out in-company training.

The primary aim of Kepner-Tregoe training is defined as 'to show managers, in a short time, how to make the process of problem analysis and decision making visible to themselves'.[19] Once the process is brought into awareness then 'the practice of skills of problem analysis' or 'what a man *does* with information' – can inspire effectiveness.

In the APEX programme, for example, fifteen or more managers spend a residential five days tackling the problems and decisions of an imaginary APEX company. There is some pre-course reading on both the Kepner-Tregoe 'content' and the 'APEX Company'. The managers meet in small groups and plenary problem sessions working from 8.30 am to 5 pm. The first evening is spent in analysing the tape-recorded sessions on the material in the light of Kepner-Tregoe 'concepts and procedures', and subsequent evenings in relating the content to the managers' own problems. Besides changing the composition of the small groups throughout the week, the course leader also rotates the managerial positions, e.g. production manager, sales manager. 'The emphasis is always on how efficiently they used the information they were given to arrive at the cause of the problem and make an appropriate decision.'[20] The course makes extensive use of feed-back or critique sessions, where the mental processes of the members as recorded on tape are compared with those recommended by Kepner and Tregoe. A variety of follow-up procedures is available after the basic one-week course.[21]

EVALUATION

In his introduction to *The Rational Manager,* Perrin Stryker referred to the authors' switch to what he called 'this engineering approach'. The phrase is an illuminating one. The Kepner-Tregoe emphasis on what elsewhere have been called 'problems of explanation' fits in well with engineering or production problems, such as breakdowns in machines or assembly lines. The liberal use of such words as 'specification' and 'precision' reinforces the engineering tone of the book. The material on decision making (as opposed to problem solving) is only a development of the now familiar five steps.

As will be seen this approach lays heavy emphasis on analysis and its close cousin, classification. The Kepner-Tregoe definition of a problem appears to be narrow, for reasons given elsewhere in this book. Significantly there is no real discussion of decisions about purpose or aims. Nor do the authors have much time for creative problem solving, although they do conclude that brainstorming can generate more possibilities or courses of action in the decision making phase. The unconscious mind does not enter into their reckoning at all. It would also be a mistake to assume that all problems can be reduced to problems of explanation, or that all decisions can be seen as responses to problems or deviations from the normal or expected. Despite these limitations the Kepner-Tregoe emphasis on the intellectual disciplines of using precise language, asking specific questions and expecting specific answers, is a valuable one for all who make decisions in any sphere.

Lateral Thinking

HISTORY

'Lateral thinking' is a phrase introduced by Edward de Bono in the mid 1960s. He holds degrees in medicine and psychology, and has written four books around the theme : *The Uses of Lateral Thinking* (1967), *The Five Day Course in Thinking* (1967), *The Mechanism of Mind* (1969) and *Lateral Thinking: A Textbook of Creativity* (1970), besides numerous articles.[22] Edward de Bono lectures internationally to a variety of industrial companies, professional societies and public service organizations who are interested in creativity.

CONTENT

Edward de Bono declared that 'vertical thinking is digging the same hole deeper : lateral thinking is realizing that you cannot dig a hole in a different hole in a different place by digging the same hole deeper. Traditionally we have always been made to use vertical thinking, in which one arrangement of information develops directly into another – just as one deepens an existing hole.' Where a problem does not yield to head-on logical attack, 'lateral thinking' teaches you to look beside, over, above or beneath it. A problem Edward de Bono defines as 'simply the difference between what one has and what one wants'.[23] Problems that require more information can be solved by logical steps; those which need 'restructuring' of available information lend themselves to 'lateral thinking'. For example :

A firm was involved in the small-scale manufacture of nitro-glycerine which involves the use of 20 per cent oleum. Unfortunately the oleum freezes at quite a high temperature. This did not matter when the process was a small-scale one for which the 40-gallon drums could be kept in a warm shed. But when the firm switched to large-scale production this meant using 3,000-gallon tanks and these had to be provided with a heating system. The heating system proved inadequate and consulting engineers had to be called in. They suggested that in order to keep the oleum warm what was required was a more efficient heating system and better lagging. This was going to be expensive.

Then a certain Mr R. Rouse had a different idea. The next stage in the process of manufacturing nitro-glycerine involves the addition of nitric acid and as soon as even a 3 per cent addition is made the freezing point is depressed. Mr Rouse suggested this be done at once and this eliminated the heating problem at a fraction of the cost.

In this example one can see the deficiences of second-stage information processing. When the problem was seen as one of keeping the oleum warm it was inevitable that some form of heating would be required. But Mr Rouse had a different first-stage approach; he thought not of keeping the oleum warm but of stopping it from freezing. And this slight change in viewpoint made a very practical difference. He was thinking laterally.[24]

'The most fundamental difference between lateral thinking and vertical thinking,' wrote Edward de Bono in his third book 'is that in vertical thinking one is not allowed to be wrong at any stage, whereas in lateral thinking one is allowed to be wrong on the way to the solution. Being wrong may be necessary in order to get information together in a certain way which can then develop into a useful solution. The solution itself must be correct, but it may be necessary to be wrong in order ever to get here.'[25]

When it comes down to 'how to do it' the three books are scattered with 'rules of thumb', such as think in visual images, predetermine the number of solutions and fill the quota deliberately, reverse the relationships of the available information, and use analogies, relating the abstract to the concrete.[26]

METHODS OF TRAINING

Lateral thinking is described as 'more a habit of mind than knowledge of some technique', and Edward de Bono believes it can be acquired by specific training. 'As in golf, a sort of general coaching would be of some use, but of much more use would be individual attention to find out in any one person the particular difficulties that interfered with the fluency of the process.'[27] *The Five Day Course in Thinking* is the author's do-it-yourself course designed to develop an awareness in the reader of his own style of thinking, its strong point and its weakness, by posing him with a number of problems involving such objects as beer bottles and table knives.

His latest book, *Lateral Thinking: A Textbook of Creativity* (1970), written for teachers and children, is 'designed to teach creativity in as deliberate a manner as mathematics or history'. Perhaps significantly this book includes material on brainstorming along with the approach and methods described in the earlier books.

EVALUATION

As to the content of Edward de Bono's four books there is little that he has to say about creative thinking (which he calls a 'more self-satisfied name' than lateral thinking) which is not to be found in the literature on the subject. Even the phrase he has coined – 'lateral thinking' – recalls Sourian's famous remark *'pour inventer il faut penser à côté'* (to invent you must think aside). His emphasis on the role played by chance in invention, for example, is paralleled by W. Gordon's chapter on 'Play and Irrelevance' in *Synectics* (1961). The material on how the mind works and the relationship of different modes of thinking (variously labelled as insight, sequential, strategic, lateral, logical, mathematical, and vertical) seems to me often confused and repetitive.

The merit of Edward de Bono's lectures and books, in my opinion, is that he can demonstrate in a visual concrete way, by using children's games and puzzles, that other than rational approaches to problems can produce useful solutions. His array of academic degrees and his own inventive mind ('Once, by fiddling with balloons, he devised a machine for doctors to test lung function ... he's invented toys and games too') certainly helps him in popularizing creative thinking. His invention of the phrase 'lateral thinking' to replace creative thinking has helped in the work of popularizing as it sounds like something new. His books contain no reference to anyone else's work on the subject. Allowing that he has an educated natural creative ability himself it has yet to be demonstrated that Edward de Bono can develop this potential in others by his do-it-yourself book method.

Conclusion

Helping people to learn to think more effectively is such a difficult business that we should not be surprised if the training courses devised so far prove to be like the proverbial curate's egg, good only in parts. There is the additional difficulty, which I should like to stress, that the written accounts upon which the above notes are based cannot convey the full flavour of the courses in question, let alone the more recent developments in content and methods that have yet to be committed to paper. We should properly regard them as experiments. Looking at their strong points and turning from the weaker or less satisfactory ones, they begin to point us towards a short course or seminar which could make available to very large numbers of people the fruits of research and experiment in applied thinking, such as they are.

CHAPTER NINE

TRAINING FOR DECISIONS

Having reviewed the main recent and current methods of training in this field it remains for me to put forward my own views. First, however, we must establish whether or not any form of training in thinking is worth undertaking. The arguments against it are considerable. It could be urged that heredity, family life, school, college or university shape our thinking entirely, that after the age of about twenty-two or twenty-three years we may go on acquiring knowledge but our basic thinking patterns, attitudes and biases are firmly and unalterably established. If you want to improve thinking, it could be urged, go to the schools or universities. Secondly, as we have noted, there is no overwhelming evidence that the courses reviewed in Chapter Eight have made a substantial and lasting difference to the thinking of those concerned, despite the faith which they may inspire.

On the other hand, there is undoubtedly a growing sense of need for courses in decision making, problem solving and creative thinking. In reply to a questionnaire that was sent to 132 firms and public organizations in connection with leadership training, over thirty were already in one or more of the three areas either using available training or attempting to teach something themselves. Therefore there is a case for saying that if training is going to be undertaken anyway it should be as good as possible.

A more substantial point stems from an analogy with leadership training. We know that the combined effects of family, school and university do not necessarily realize the overall potential for leadership that exists within this country or any other. Short courses in leadership have certainly revealed this fact, not only in the management field but in almost every other occupation where people come together to work in groups and organizations. May it not be that there is much latent mental or intellectual potential? Since we all have 10,000 million brain-cells, is it not possible that the odd 100 million are either idle or underused?

This suspicion is reinforced when we recollect that many outstanding thinkers, not only in the leadership of industry but also in science and the arts, did not shine at school or university. It has been fashionable to call them slow developers. This is partly true, but it may also be that for many people it takes the triggers of real problems and decisions to spark off major thinking responses. Thus intellectual development, or learning how to think, may continue throughout our lives. Therefore in theory people should always be willing to learn more about thinking, and this is what we find in practice.

My own experience is confined largely to training leaders, and this provides the context for the course proposed and described in the following pages. Just to hold a 'how to think' course without such a context seems to me too diffuse to be much more than a waste of time. But related to a wider programme of leadership development some instruction in applied thinking can make a most valuable contribution. Naturally (like most courses) it would have to summarize, place in order and build upon what the students know already, but it would serve a purpose by setting this knowledge firmly in the leadership context and by giving intellectual development a new direction.

The hour-glass model of thinking contexts

To illustrate the part that a short course in thinking might play in a leadership development programme it is necessary to recapitulate the possible major phases of our intellectual development.

At a relatively early age, partly by inherited preference and partly by environment, the more able child begins to apply or exercise his power of analysis, synthesis and valuing within the broad context of either the arts or sciences. At school he remains a generalist within that context; the future physicist, for example, may still be tackling chemical or biological problems, while the historian still copes with literary or linguistic ones. This extended field may be maintained in the first year or two at university, but eventually the mind begins to focus down on to a particular subject, and then to a small area within it. The minds tends to follow a line of least resistance down the branches of knowledge until it finds a specialized twig upon which it can perch with least discomfort. We could call this the process of 'problem area narrowing'. In its last stages it is characterized by a large technical expertise in solving problems which is not transferable to other twigs, let alone branches, of knowledge.

For progress in occupational areas where leadership is necessary, however, a complementary process of 'problem area widening' has to take place : the specialist must give way to the generalist. Of course, the context for applied thinking in other occupations can also widen : the tax-specialist barrister may become a judge, for example. But the tendency is marked in what could be called organizational careers. Thus the characteristic shape of problem-solving areas at different points in a person's career (including school) often resembles an hour-glass or egg-timer. Had not the terms already been appropriated by psychologists for other uses we could perhaps have called the bottom and top shapes convergence and divergence. It is important to know where the students are in the hour-glass for it is the direction they are moving which provides the immediate setting for a course.

For example, M. L. Johnson Abercrombie caught the medical students at a stage of narrowing from general science subjects to particular problems appropriate to the medical field, such as interpreting the evidence of X-rays. We may posit that leaders or managers at the junior level, as part of their initiation into a particular occupational field, need specialized training in the characteristic decision-making and problem-solving situations they will either be facing already or will be shortly so doing. We should also expect a high heuristic content : the rules of thumb, clues, hints or tips which have to be picked up on the job or from those close to it.

At this first stage broad considerations concerning the nature of thinking or general principles would have little intrinsic appeal. Rather the student would respond to demonstrations of the importance of inspecting the evidence, determining what type or kind of problem it is, and applying the appropriate solution, rule or principle. The latter have to be as specific and concrete as possible. Simplifications, answers, or short-cuts are sought : anything that works in the specialized thought area.

In keeping with this preoccupation, educational courses which by their nature often tend to introduce the general in the form of abstract language or theory are only bearable (let alone seen to be valuable) if they include simulations of the concrete problem areas upon which the students are focusing down. The counterpart of Dr Abercrombie's X-rays in management training courses are the now-familiar business case-studies. A high degree of realism is necessary, otherwise the case-study will be rejected.

This description helps to explain the fact that business schools such as Harvard which rely heavily on the case-study method have tended to include little or no general theory about decision making or problem solving with the case-studies. Practice on large numbers of cases under the tutelage of a professor in the particular sub-field, such as marketing, represents the appropriate intellectual training. The tips or clues which are presumably imported are so highly adapted to the sub-field as to be nontransferable in any way.

Once the narrowest part of the hour-glass is passed and the context for thinking begins to widen outwards, some more general training becomes appropriate. In many careers, including all managerial ones, this coincides with the beginnings of real leadership responsibilities. Although these may be bounded still within a certain technical context the social dimension has already made its appearance on the stage. With it comes a gradual weighting in the importance of decision making as opposed to problem solving. Within decision making itself the interest and emphasis begin to cluster around the purpose-aims-objectives complex rather than choosing the best means. This leads eventually to a deeper interest in the valuing aspect of thinking among senior leaders.

Almost at any stage in this widening of mental focus a seminar or course which sets out to look at applied thinking in more general terms will be perceived as relevant. It could be argued, however, that despite their relatively narrow focused work setting younger men and women would be better recipients than older ones. Not only do they tend to have a natural mental flexibility, but they also need fairly early on in a leadership-orientated career an inoculation against specialization. On the other hand, older and more senior men will grasp more readily what the course is about. Balancing these considerations, and allowing for some career structure discrepancies between organizations, we might conclude that the optimum age range is roughly twenty-five to forty years. This does not mean, however, that training will be ineffective or valueless outside this span. Indeed, we need much more experiment and research in the effects of such training on schoolchildren and university students at one end of the scale, and boards of directors at the other.

Theory and practice

Before describing the design of actual training it is necessary to make clear some of the general considerations, assumptions and principles upon which it has been based. For in the long run these are more important than specific embodiments, which will always be shaped by such factors as the age, background and working situation of the course members, and the training context of the given course or programme.

Most training can be seen as a dialogue between theory and practice. Theory is used here not to denote a speculative hypothesis but more 'the general laws, principles or causes of something known or observed' (*Shorter Oxford English Dictionary*). The emphasis in theory falls upon what is held to be general rather than particular. Consequently it must necessarily be expressed in abstract language or forms. In contrast practice means the performance or doing of something, especially customary or constant action. It can also mean the exercise of any art or craft with the purpose of attaining proficiency. Here the emphasis falls upon doing in a particular action or sequence of them.

We all know that it is the interaction of theory and practice which brings progress in the exercise of any science, art or craft. One without the other is impoverished. Consequently it is especially important when either appraising or designing courses to look most carefully at the general ideas that are being put over explicitly or implicitly. The student or course member should have the opportunity to relate the theory in question to more than one case, and also to examine a number of cases in the light of the given theory. If possible the relating of the two should be done by the student himself, so that the teacher's job is to engineer juxtapositions of theory and practice rather than spell out their inter-relationship. The gap between theory and practice, or general and particular, may have to be widened or narrowed according to what might be called the 'span of relevance' of the students, for the distance of leap which the spark of understanding can make varies with individuals. Not all of us could see a connection, as did Newton's mind, between a tumbling apple and a falling moon.[1]

Lastly, the interaction of theory and practice on the course must be so conducted that it facilitates what psychologists call transfer : the ability to relate the same general ideas gained in education or training to characteristic or unique situations at work in such a way that the person now operates more effectively within them. Transfer is an aspect of our natural learning ability, and it tends to happen of its own accord. Some transfers, including negative ones, from situation to situation will thus almost automatically take place, but positive ones can be encouraged and promoted if the right mediating exercises are introduced as mental links, like stepping-stones set at ever-wider intervals across a river. Prior to that much also depends upon the way in which the theory is consigned to the depth minds of the students. If it is received with interest and instant recognition of value, and reinforced by some early successful applications, it will tend to suggest itself naturally when the signals or cues in later real situations play the particular combination or pattern of notes required to summon it from the unconscious.

Course aim and objectives

The overall aim of any course in this area would be to improve the effectiveness of thinking in the senses defined by the phrases decision making, problem solving and creative thinking. This aim could be broken down into the following objectives : to give the students concerned an opportunity to think for themselves about the intellectual aspects of their work; to present them with a model of thinking which will cause them directly or indirectly to improve their own abilities as applied thinkers; and to help them to work out a strategy for making fuller use of their mental faculties.

An experimental course

In 1970 Whitbreads Ltd, the brewery firm employing over 15,000 people, invited the author to lead a series of three short courses for middle managers on the ground covered by this book. About twenty managers ranging in age from twenty- to fifty-year-olds took part on each occasion. The course was preceded by one general day on the behavioural sciences in industry and two days of leadership training in a form evolved earlier by the author. The sessions on thinking occupied all Thursday and the beginning of Friday, but most of this last morning of the course was reserved for revision, project-planning and evaluation.

SESSION I : THE NATURE OF THINKING

After a brief introduction relating the forthcoming sessions to the three-circle model of leadership[2] and stressing the importance of effective thinking in management, the course members were divided into syndicates and asked to report back in twenty minutes with the answers written up on newsprint on the wall to the following questions : what is decision making? what is problem solving? what is creative thinking?

From the general discussion on the reports (which are left up on a wall throughout the course) the need to clarify the nature of thinking emerged. This led to short definitions and an exposition of the main elements of thinking, namely analysis, synthesis and valuing. It was also explained that these activities operate at different levels : the first introduction to the concept of the depth mind. As one cannot talk about the depth mind without images or metaphors I used three : thinking was compared to an iceberg (which enabled me to comment upon the false dichotomy between thought and emotion), the passage of a submarine, and the workings of a computer.

Thirdly, in this presentation of general ideas (which took no more than twenty minutes with questions from the audience), I turned to the topic of decision making and highlighted the necessity of being clear about what one wants to do. As an example of useful analysis and classification, the breakdown of purpose, aims and objectives (see page 52) was offered to the course members. Before stopping for coffee they were told that at the start of the next session they would go straight into syndicates to work out in discussion an example of an *objective,* three *aims* for a brewery and the *purpose* of industry.

SESSION 2 : DECISION MAKING

After thirty minutes the syndicates returned with their reports, and once again their findings were compared. Usually the first question posed no difficulty, but the second caused more discussion, and the third proved to be very much harder to answer satisfactorily.

The answers served to illustrate how values and the attitudes based on them enter into management decision making at all its levels, just as they colour all human thinking. (This point is reinforced if course members are asked to rate the answers in order of preference, each working individually from the displayed reports. Then the ratings given to the proposed ends of industry are compared.)[3]

Then attention was turned to the remaining aspects of decision making; the five phases (see page 51), and the possible distortions were briefly explained with the help of a duplicated version of them in everyone's hands. Course members were asked to produce examples of decision making from their own experience which either illustrated the phases or demonstrated what happens when they are ignored. It was emphasized that this was a model of what happens, and that it was much more tidy than real life decision making.

After an hour of discussion it is useful to field a case study as a practical illustration of the points already made. On two of the courses I have used the example of General Eisenhower's decision about airborne landings for D-Day, 1944. Although the background is military, which can be seen as a disadvantage, it certainly generates discussion on 'points of no return'. It was presented in two parts, the first ending after Leigh-Mallory's conversation with Eisenhower (see page 33). With this open ending before them the course members were asked to decide what they would do if they were in General Eisenhower's shoes. Then the second part was given to them and discussed in plenary session.

SESSION 3 : DECISIONS AND PROBLEMS

This session, lasting only one hour, begins with a short talk in plenary session on the relation between decisions and problems. Problems are seen primarily as obstacles 'thrown forwards' or in front of the leader as he sets out towards a goal. Careful plans with a built-in degree of flexibility can lessen the likelihood of problems emerging. But some will almost certainly crop up in the chosen path, and may be regarded as challenges to the intellectual powers of the manager.

At this point the twenty-seven minute Richard Costain colour film *Critical Path* was sometimes shown to illustrate decision making about the best means for a given end; to indicate how problems can to some extent be predicted, and analysed in advance in terms of the whole operation and to serve as an example of the newer techniques available to managers (see Appendix 1).

SESSION 4 : PROBLEM SOLVING

The session began with about twenty minutes work on three puzzles. These were mainly to stimulate or warm up the thinking of course members. They are open to different interpretations, and the tutor is not advised to spend too long on them. They can serve as pegs on which to hang some general points, however, and thus recall the course to the fundamental two-way traffic between concrete cases and general ideas.

For the benefit of the general reader, here are the three problems for you to test your wits on :

NINE DOTS

Put nine dots on a piece of paper in the form of a square and equidistant from each other :

Now join them with four straight continuous lines.

SIX MATCHES

Take six matches and spread them on the table in front of you. From them make four equilateral triangles.

WHO OWNS THE ZEBRA?

There are five houses, each with a front door of a different colour, and inhabited by men of different nationalities, with different pets and drinks. Each man smokes a different kind of pipe tobacco.

The Englishman lives in the house with the red door.

The Spaniard owns the dog.

Coffee is drunk in the house with the green door.

The Ukrainian drinks tea.

The house with the green door is immediately to the right (*your* right) of the house with the ivory door.

The Medium Cut smoker owns snails.

Spun Cut is smoked in the house with the yellow door.

Milk is drunk in the middle house.

The Norwegian lives in the first house on the left.

The man who smokes Mixture lives in the house next to the man with the fox.

Spun Cut is smoked in the house next to the house where the horse is kept.

The Flake smoker drinks orange juice.

The Japanese smokes Rough Cut.

The Norwegian lives next to the house with the blue door.

Now, who drinks water? And who owns the zebra?

(Solutions on p. 148)

With the first two puzzles an alternative from doing them in plenary session is to divide into syndicates and let one person tackle them, talking aloud while he does so, while the remaining four observe and take notes on his thought processes.

The second part of the session consisted of a twenty-minute exposition of the problem-solving stages relevant in 'closed system' situations, where the way to the solution of the problem lay in diagnosing the cause of certain unwanted effects. Without ruling out the possibility that flair or intuition will short-circuit the process, the advantages of a systematic or logical approach are pointed out. At the heart of such step-by-step analysis lies the discipline of comparing similarities and dissimilarities in a number of cases in order to determine causes for the problematic 'unlike' effect.

In the last part of the session the course members are asked to apply this approach to a case study, the 'Paint Spray Gun Exercise' (see Appendix 3).

SESSION 5 : CREATIVE THINKING

In the second and third courses I began this session with the rusty pipe experiment. On my table in front of the audience (arranged as for all the sessions in an open-sided square) I placed a two inch rusty pipe some twenty inches in length, mounted vertically on a two inch square wooden base. Clearing my papers and the water jug tray to one end, I arranged on the table the experimental implements : a wire coat-hanger, pliers, saw, a piece of string thirty inches in length, some chewing gum, a broom, miscellaneous weights, hooks and two sheets of cardboard.

The course are then told that there is a table tennis ball trapped in the bottom of the pipe. Their task is to see how to get it out without turning the pipe upside down using the materials on the table in the shortest time. Working individually they were given two minutes to write down their solutions. They were free to inspect the materials at close range within that two minutes. Their solutions were then collected. The course was then given three minutes in groups of five to work out a solution, and these answers were also collected up. (For the answer see page 149.)

The experiment leads into a short fifteen minute talk on the nature and process of creative thinking, which in the higher reaches of the continuum bears the fruit of original thought and new inventions. Creative thinking involves making new syntheses at the various levels of the mind. Can you be trained to think creatively at any point on the continuum from fresh or novel thinking to original creative thinking widely-recognized for its quality in a given field? There is no firm evidence to suppose so, but to some extent the factors militating against creative thinking can be located and assaulted.

At this point, after a brief explanation of the appropriate rules, the course are asked to brainstorm twenty new uses for a common object, such as a brick or a barrel, which is placed on a table in the centre.

Besides introducing the role of groups in productive thinking the exercise is used to demonstrate a way of attacking two barriers to creative thinking, the first of which is functional fixedness, or the perception of reality in the structure which first presents itself to the mind. The other barrier is premature criticism, or a confusion amounting to civil war between the valuing and synthesizing attributes of the mind.

After discussion of these points a further exercise took place in which three common objects were placed on the table, and the course (working in syndicates) were invited to synthesize them with one other object of their own choice into a new whole which could be marketed. In addition they had to name the new product and firm, and suggest a target group of customers for its marketing operations in the first year.

The session concluded with a summary of research into creative thinking and with some further suggestions for putting the depth mind to work.

SESSION 6 : DECISIONS ABOUT PEOPLE

This session took place after supper. It was designed not so much to teach as to highlight an area for further reflection and study. In the introduction, the growing importance of good judgement about people as one becomes a more senior manager was stressed. The lack of precision in our language on qualities and traits was noted. Analysis, synthesis and valuing all come into play when we start thinking about people, either in general or in particular. There is room for creative thinking as well. Leadership is often most creative in and through its decisions about people, both for their lives and for the enterprise. Several examples were given to buttress the point.

As a principle it is suggested that the hard part of judgement is predicting how a person will behave in the future. Classifying what we observe of people in terms of qualities or traits is an indispensable (if most imprecise) way of communicating information about people. Yet we have to be cautious of accepting such classifications as ready-made predictions. Most managers rely initially upon the history of a person balanced (and eventually outweighed) by their experience of him.

To illustrate how we naturally collect and arrange evidence about people into patterns from which we then (correctly or incorrectly) make inferences or extrapolate future likely behaviour, the film *Twelve Angry Men* is employed as an exercise. Just before the first formal vote in the jury room is taken the film is stopped and the course members are asked to predict the order in which the eleven jurymen will change their opinions from 'guilty' to 'not guilty'. Often the exercise ends with some useful discussion of the relationship of groups and individuals in decision making. The group pressures first brought to bear upon the architect played by Henry Fonda (who incidentally is alone shown as employing a visual and spatial imagination) by the other eleven jurors, and upon others later in the film, highlight some of the potential dangers inherent in corporate decisions. On the other hand, the dictum that two heads are better than one – and three better than two – seems to be borne out when it comes to judgements about people. How far should the manager share his decisions over people, or indeed over any other matter? This question leads into the social dimension of managerial decision making, which was tackled in the next session.

SESSION 7 : SHARING DECISIONS AND CONCLUSION

In the final session Tannenbaum and Schmidt continuum (see page 66) is presented and discussed with the object of clarifying the factors which should be present in the leader's surface mind, on the fringes of consciousness or in his depth mind, when he comes to decide how far or in what ways he should share a decision. Some idea of the appropriate waveband of decision participation for a particular field of work should also emerge from the discussions.

The course ends with a recapitulation of the main points made in the past sessions, and advice on follow-up work. In all courses this would include suggestions for further reading. In the case of Whitbreads, where the course members were going to undertake project work before meeting their tutors again in six months' time, the relation of the applied thinking sessions of the week's course to the projects was also explored.

Summary

In this chapter some possible general training principles have been illustrated by the concrete example of three courses held for a British company in 1970. The sessions, individually or in small groupings, have also been tried out and tested on a number of other courses, ranging from one with eighty Anglican bishops in Boston USA (1963) to those involving young managers from a wide spectrum of organizations on Industrial Society courses and seminars. These sessions have aroused much interest, and they are generally enjoyed and subjectively assessed highly by participants in written course evaluations. But it is too early to attempt any more systematic evaluation, not least because we know too little about the possible criteria or methods for such judgements. Until that day this form of training in programmes, courses and seminars will still have to be judged in terms of cost-effectiveness by the sponsors of the course, who must partly base their verdict on the verdict of the course members, which will need to be interpreted with experience.

CONCLUSION

Despite the vast literature on thinking no general theory has been put forward and accepted which takes account of the main variables concerned. Consequently there is often a wide discrepancy between how we actually think ourselves and the formulae or recipes recommended by the text-books and articles on the subject. In this book I have suggested that any model would have to include the following facets : analysing, synthesizing, valuing; depth mind activity; emotional colouring; the 'people dimension'; and the 'hourglass' theory of focus.

Taken together these dimensions begin to give us a model of the raw material of applied thinking. Too often we conceive thinking to be only or mainly analysis. There are some who believe that our lopsided educational systems have been to blame in that respect, and by the introduction of synthesizing approaches, such as project work, have sought to redress the balance. Be that as it may, we certainly need a wider and deeper understanding of the nature of thinking, and more bold experiments in methods of teaching at all levels of education.

This does not mean that some of the pre-packaged constructs of these facets of thinking, such as the so-called logical approach to decision making (the five steps, or variants of them) or the scientific method of problem solving are worthless. On the contrary, the methodical or text-book approaches may prove useful in certain situations. Moreover, like musical scales, playing them can give the mind some practice in arranging the basic themes and exploring their relationships to each other.

Avoiding such constructs, as advocated in this book, does not necessarily imply that there are no disciplines in thinking, no need to strive for method and precision. Thinking is neither intrinsically easy nor difficult; it is natural. It is the function of art to improve upon nature. Like a horse, the natural energy of thinking has to be broken in, but not broken down. The best thinkers seem to be those who have subjected themselves, or have been subjected, to a rigorous intellectual training, and then have been allowed to revert to their natural state. They have risen upwards and outwards, so to speak, through the narrow neck of the hourglass.

We should therefore be suspicious of any courses in management studies which promise rapid improvements in decision making or problem solving, and especially of those which offer instant creativity. Often such courses flourish upon what they should be trying to remedy : the atrophied valuing attribute of human thinking. We are perhaps least good at value thinking, mainly because values are like calories in our food : we do not see them. Certainly effective thinking in any sphere requires a great deal of work. We see this notably in those who are consistently original : long years of preparation and sharpening of wits lies behind the sudden illuminations or flashes of intuition. Indeed, more than once it has been suggested that persistence is the most common characteristic of great thinkers. Like Jacob wrestling with the unknown angel, the thinker seems to be saying, 'I will not let you go, unless you bless me.'[1]

Yet within this struggle towards order, clarity, truth, the mind is not necessarily tense or strained. Like an archer, the mind hits its mark partly by pulling and partly by letting go. Without a willing depth mind which he both feeds and trusts, a person's thinking will be impoverished, it will lack depth. Samuel Taylor Coleridge made much the same point :

> Most of my readers will have observed a small water-insect on the surface of rivulets, which throws a cinque-spotted shadow fringed with prismatic colours on the sunny bottom of the brook; and will have noticed, how the little animal *wins* its way up the stream by alternate pulses of active and passive motion, now resisting the current, and now yielding to it in order to gather strength and a momentary *fulcrum* for a further propulsion. This is no unapt emblem of the mind's self-experience in the act of thinking.[2]

These considerations present some cliff-face obstacles to the teacher, college lecturer or management trainer, and in our present state of knowledge he can be forgiven for believing them to be insurmountable. Yet the situation is not as hopeless as that. If it is true that most of us have latent unused potential for thinking, such understanding of the mind and the rough illustrations of its workings as we now possess can have a dramatic effect in encouraging us to persevere upon our own intellectual adventure. Nor should we be too critical of those who are already seeking to bring about this inward release of energy and enthusiasm, for, as the proverb declares, 'In the country of the blind the one-eyed man is king.'

We may take encouragment from the widening consensus that in general people have a natural desire to learn and grow. Curiosity, fashioned into more enduring interests, is the appetite of the human mind. If we follow those interests they can lead us to what we need at any given time. Yet the higher reaches of creative thinking, the peaks of great decisions and the riddles which stand like sentinels around the heart of the universe, will only yield to those who face and overcome the torments of the unknown. As Sherpa Tensing, conqueror of Everest, once remarked : 'It is with God as with mountains, he must be approached without fear.'

F

APPENDIX 1

SOME TECHNIQUES FOR MANAGERS

Many of the recent books and articles with decision making in their titles turn out to be concerned with highly specialized techniques of problem solving. These practical and tangible methods of sorting out certain kinds of recurrent problems have an obvious appeal, but it is a mistake to confuse them with the total mental activity required of a manager, as some over-enthusiastic advocates seem to imply. As they tend to lead us too far into the field of specific problems it is not part of the aim of this book to describe them in any detail, but it is necessary for completeness to outline them. The terminology is constantly changing, which makes any definitive statement difficult at present.

Network Analysis, Critical Path Method (CPM) and Programme Evaluation and Review (PERT)

These are similar methods of grasping the planning problem of a project by analysing it into its component parts and recording them on a network model or diagram, which can then be used for controlling the inter-relating activities necessary to complete the project. The essence of the method is that the necessary analysis of the problem can best be done on a two-dimensional plan. The analysis identifies the objective as a clear end-result, the constituent activities and events, the last two shown respectively as lines and circles. In building a house, for example, an activity would be plumbing or plastering, and an event the completion of the foundations or the delivery of the bricks.

Network Analysis, PERT and CPM, although once rather different techniques, have converged, and are now almost synonymous. They can fruitfully be used to solve any problem involving space/time planning when a definite end-result can be envisaged : for example, writing a book, setting up a new department, construction work of all kinds, getting married, cooking the breakfast, installing a data processing system, or merging two organizations.

Operational Research (OR)

Operational research is the name given to the method of examining operational problems in organizations, notably problems where the key factors can be expressed as mathematical formulae. As a term it has gradually come to embrace all the techniques described in this Appendix. The techniques employed in operational research usually have a mathematical or statistical basis. Recurrent managerial problems in this category include 'allocation problems'. These involve the assigning of limited resources to a number of activities to achieve maximum results, The classic example, which gave rise to Operational Research in World War Two, was how to use most effectively a fleet of bombers from various bases in Britain against a number of targets in Germany. The same OR method has been employed to work out the optimum use of lorries in the transport of goods from a variety of depots to retail points.

More recent recurrent problems to be studied under this heading include 'inventory depletion', where research seeks to establish rules for issuing stocks, especially perishable or semi-perishable ones, and 'inventory replenishment and production control', where it has attempted to find the most effective 'trigger' (level, time, demand, or a combination of them) for ordering replenishments.

'Queuing problems' involved waiting periods. For example, to what extent times will be increased if the arrival rate of customers goes up by ten per cent? By what methods (such as stock levels) could the original waiting time be restored? So far it has been reported that only a small percentage of the published research papers are of any practical use.

In operational research problems are characteristically analysed not by two-dimensional charts, such as network analysis, but by constructing models of mathematical equations between elements that are controllable by management and those which are not. 'The values of the elements can be varied in a series of experiments using simulation (i.e. computer simulation) or mathematical analysis, until the combination of controllable values is found which is likely to give the best results having regard to the object to be achieved, e.g. the quickest or the cheapest method of delivering goods.' Preparing material of a computer simulation exercise enforces clear logical analysis. Consequently many problems get solved before they reach the computer.

On the whole, operational research lends itself to problems where the values concerned are quantifiable, such as money and time. Unfortunately, these are rarely the most difficult or challenging of the problems the manager or anyone else encounters in his daily life. Even such an apparently clear-cut variable as cost can be extremely difficult to quantify in any way acceptable by the mathematician.

In the last few years OR (as it has come to be known) has become more of an 'umbrella' term, embracing the previous section as well as the subsequent section at least as far as its practitioners are concerned. Although forays have been made into the areas of manpower planning, finance, and advertising (choosing the media), most firms use their OR departments for company logistics in one form or another. GKN, a large group of companies in the engineering industry manufacturing a wide variety of steel products, serves as an example, as this report by D. J. Spurrell, published in the *Journal of the Association of Teachers of Management* (Vol. I, Pt 1, 1970) makes clear :

> The assignments have been concerned with the control of stocks, both of raw materials and as finished products; with production planning, often integrated with finished stock control; the forecasting and planning of raw materials and tool requirements, etc. Even in areas where, ostensibly, marketing problems were to be tackled, the problems have turned out to be concerned with the distribution and holding of finished stocks. The following are examples of work that has been carried out in the past two or three years.
>
> PRODUCTION PLANNING : The design and implementation of a system of forecasting, replenishing stock and planning production for a manufacturer of engineering fasteners. The system was based upon the monthly reorder of items grouped together in families determined by the major set-up costs. Variations of product, for example, of length, within the family were made only at small extra cost, giving the flexibility of smaller quantities for any one item. The frequency of any item in the family

'make' was determined by the rate of demand; the manufacturing quantities were based upon reorder interval rules.

PURCHASING POLICIES : There have been several studies examining the purchasing policies to be adopted in various fields of raw materials and fuels. In most of these examples, the price savings achievable through buying quantities attracting discounts is balanced against the usage of the materials in question and against the increase in holding costs. Fairly simple reordering rules have been devised and operated by the existing sales staff without additional support in several cases. It has also been possible to generate a profile of purchasing quantities, so that week by week, the actual purchasing performance can be monitored to determine whether the buyers are doing a good job or not.

MATERIALS HANDLING : Several studies have been carried out concerning the movement of material. In a new factory, the plant layout has been determined and tested by the use of simulation techniques. Simulation was also used to investigate the handling of all materials into and within a large works.

STORAGE LOCATION : Other assignments have studied the distribution and storage of finished parts or components, particularly when companies have operated branches.

CO-ORDINATION OF PRODUCTION : One of the most difficult and interesting assignments has been a large exercise to investigate the problems of co-ordinating production and stock policies for three independently operating companies, which however were linked together in a vertical chain of operations. While each single company can be well managed to achieve its individual company objectives, many instances occurred with particular products which suggested that the Group as a whole could benefit by closer co-ordination of the three companies concerned. Because of the size, the number of products and the complexity of the operations, it proved very difficult to study this problem item by item. An aggregate approach was adopted and the flows of aggregated products and information were examined in some detail, using the techniques of industrial dynamics. The model was run on the IBM 7904 using the DYNAMO programme. By the standards set up earlier, this has probably been the least effective assignment. However, one result of the Steering Committee meetings involving the three companies has been that regular meetings are now being held by their respective production planning staffs.

Decision trees, decision theory, preference theory

Decision trees (*alias* decision theory, or preference theory) is an adaptation of network analysis to problems where there is un-certainty, and where possible outcomes can be given a financial value. In other words, it is typically suited to examining financial investment problems in such a way as to reveal the most preferable course of action.

As in network analysis a network or tree is drawn up showing the relationships of the series of possible decisions and events, the 'courses of action' of the military appreciation. The probability of each outcome must then be assessed and the financial reward of each one calculated. Maximum pay-off and probability of outcome tend to be in inverse ratio, as any punter at the race courses will verify. The aim of decision trees, however, is to reduce this two-dimensional choice problem of financial reward/probability of out-come to a single one. Preference defines the subjective factor of how far you are prepared to accept greater uncertainty for greater expected profit (expected profit is worked out by multiplying the outcome by the probability of it occurring). For example, if the payoff is £10 and the chance of getting it is 0.5 (as if you tossed a coin) then the expected profit is £5.

Even so-called simple decision trees tend to be extremely elaborate, replete with mathematical formulae, scientific tables and sub-diagrams. Like all perennial attempts to work out systems for winning the football pools, busting the bookmakers or breaking the bank at Monte Carlo, these methods have yet to prove their worth as unaided producers of the right answers. But as a means of help-ing the manager to explore, examine and analyse a problem of making money when there are different courses open, each with its incumbent uncertainties and levels of expected financial yield, decision trees certainly have their place in the modern armoury of management techniques.

Games theory

Games theory is a distant cousin of so-called decision theory. Whereas decision trees deal with natural events, the theory of games is concerned with problems where the solutions will depend upon the joint result of choices made independently by two or more people. Chess, battles and a take-over struggle are such situations. Unfortunately, the theory of games at present only really helps in the limited situation of the game proper where time limits of moves are set and where outcomes can be weighted accurately. Games theory cannot be applied to open situations, such as industrial competition, military encounters or industrial relations. Consequently it tends to be of most interest to academic philosophers and psychologists, and only a stimulant to others engaged in the dialogue areas of problem solving.

Further reading
Management Decision-Making, ed. G. Yewdall, Pan Books, 1969.
Decision Making, The British Broadcasting Corporation, 1967. A collection of papers by R. J. Audley, R. B. Braithwaite, R. Cassen, J. Johnston, L. Joy, A. Rapoport, P. Self and J. W. N. Watkins.
New Decision-Making Tools for Managers: Mathematical Programming as an Aid in Solving Business Problems, ed. E. C. Bursk and J. F. Chapman, Harvard University Press, 1963.
Decision-Making: Selected Readings, ed. W. Edwards and A. Tversky, Penguin, 1967.
C. M. Berners-Lee, *Models for Decisions,* English University Press, 1965.
A. Kaufman, *The Science of Decision-Making: An Introduction to Praxeology,* Weidenfeld and Nicolson, 1968.
M. J. Sargeaunt, *Operational Research for Management,* Heinemann, 1965.
G. L. S. Shackle, *Decision Order and Time in Human Affairs,* Cambridge University Press, second edition, 1969.

APPENDIX 2

PUZZLE PROBLEMS
(see page 133)

Nine Dots

The solution is as follows :

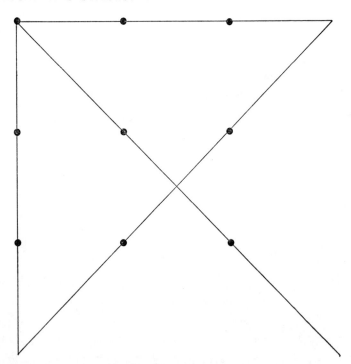

If you failed to solve the problem ask yourself why. It may be
that you assumed the lines had to be drawn *within* the boundary
of the nine dots, although that limitation was not laid down. The

puzzle may serve to illustrate also that sometimes a solution may be outside the closed frameworks our minds often impose on reality.

Six matches

Form the matches into a pyramid. The problem cannot be solved on one plane alone; you have to break out into three dimensions. Karl Duncker first used this problem in the 1920s. It is possible to argue that those who solve it easily have spatial imaginations, i.e. they can think easily of shapes, spaces and their relations to each other in three dimensions, but this does not detract from its value. Used immediately after the nine dots it is interesting to note whether or not students can see any relation between them.

Who owns the zebra?

The Norwegian drinks water.
The Japanese owns the Zebra.
It is worked out as follows :

FRONT DOORS	Yellow	Blue	Red	Ivory	Green
INHABITANTS	Norwegian	Ukrainian	Englishman	Spaniard	Japanese
PETS	Fox	Horse	Snails	Dog	**Zebra**
DRINKS	**Water**	Tea	Milk	Orange Juice	Coffee
TOBACCO	Spun Cut	Mixture	Medium Cut	Flake	Rough Cut

Rusty pipe experiment

The simplest and most elegant solution is to float the ball out using the water in the jug. This exercise can illustrate vividly the points about 'functional fixedness' made above in Chapter Five.

Further Reading

Similar problems, including some suitable for use in educational and training courses, may be found in Martin Gardner, *Mathematical Puzzles and Diversions* and *More Mathematical Puzzles and Diversions* (Penguin Books edition, 1965 and 1966); H. E. Dudeney, *Puzzles and Curious Problems*, and *More Puzzles and Curious Problems*, Fontana, 1970.

APPENDIX 3

PROBLEM SOLVING EXERCISE: THE PAINT SPRAY GUN

One of the following briefs is given to each of the five members of the working syndicates into which the course is divided for the purpose of the exercise.

Brief 1

You are Bill Johnson, the general manager, cleaning and maintenance division, London Council; you have received several complaints from your area supervisor about paint spray guns failing to work. You have decided to investigate.

You have called together the London Area Supervisor, Joe Davis, and three of the paint mechanics to try and sort it out. Their names are Fred Slater, John Hunter and David Whittaker. Each of you has some information which relates to the problem. It is up to you in calling together this meeting to ask the right questions in order to bring out the relevant information. (You are not entitled to ask the members of the meeting to read from the notes they have in front of them. You and the members of the group may only reply to specific questions.)

You have twenty minutes to solve the problem.

Brief 2

MECHANIC I — FRED SLATER

You have prepared these rough notes in preparation for the meeting which your boss Joe Davis, the area supervisor, has arranged with the general manager, Bill Johnson. Your fellow mechanics, John Hunter and David Whittaker, will also be there. The purpose of the meeting is to discuss and solve the problems with paint spray guns of which you and your colleagues have complained to the area supervisor.

'All paint guns are of same make. I checked all the faulty ones and could find nothing wrong mechanically, perfectly sound. We have had complaints from Chelsea, Richmond and all over London, can't see anything helpful there. All the mechanics were checked on their operating ability and found to be using the guns correctly. We did have to pull them up about the rust condition but apparently that was caused by the thinner paint we used to use. So mechanics all over London are having the same problem, always in the mornings when we do most of our work – the lads like to knock off early.'

Brief 3

MECHANIC 2 – JOHN HUNTER

You have prepared these rough notes in preparation for the meeting which your boss, Joe Davis, the Area Supervisor, has arranged with the General Manager, Bill Johnson. Your fellow mechanics Fred Slater and David Whittaker will also be there. The purpose of the meeting is to discuss and solve the problems with paint spray guns of which you and your colleagues have complained to the Area Supervisor.

'I've really checked those spray guns with a fine toothcomb. Nothing wrong with the handles or switches, just that the nozzles get blocked. I've only noticed complaints when we've been using white and red paint; perhaps that's significant. We really follow a strict routine – can't think when we made the mistake. The boys clean the guns in the morning – Jenners paint thinner, screw the parts together, lubricate them – Duttons oil and then pack them ready for use; in the evening they are very carefully unpacked and replaced in the shed where they are all stored.'

Brief 4

MECHANIC 3 – DAVID WHITTAKER

You have prepared these rough notes in preparation for the meeting which your boss, Joe Davis, the Area Supervisor, has arranged with the General Manager, Bill Johnson. Your fellow mechanics Fred Slater and John Hunter will also be there. The purpose of the meeting is to discuss and solve the problems with paint spray guns of which you and your colleagues have complained to the Area Supervisor.

'I've checked with paint suppliers, we get our red and white paint from Samuels and the green and blue from Lennox, but

Samuels couldn't think of any reason why the paint should be blocking the guns. Certainly all the spray guns in use have had this same complaint of becoming blocked. I did notice that all the guns seemed to have rusted a fair bit. We can't revert to brushes – takes too much time. It would be too expensive to replace the guns before we discover what the problem is.'

Brief 5

AREA SUPERVISOR – JOE DAVIS

You have been receiving complaints from your mechanics on paint spray guns failing to work. You have sent your general manager, Bill Johnson, the enclosed letter and you are about to go to the meeting he has arranged with yourself and your three mechanics, Fred Slater, John Hunter and David Whittaker to discuss the problem. Here are some notes you have made.

'Those guns were all bought at the same time, three months ago. We've contacted the suppliers and they can't think of any fault. The guns in fact came from different batches. We checked with Bristol Corporation who are using some guns from the same batches, they reported using blue and white paint all over the city with no trouble. Incidentally they use a paint thinner we gave up a couple of months ago – Good to be one jump ahead.

'I tried out the blue and green paint in the spray guns (comes from different manufacturer from red and white) but it clogged all the same.'

24 March 1970

Dear Mr Johnson,

Sorry to bring this to your notice but we've been having some trouble with the paint spray guns recently.

Over the last three weeks I have received complaints from every one of my mechanics. For example, one of my mechanics complained that his gun refused to operate when two weeks ago he painted over the new phone-boxes in Whitehall.

Another gave the same complaint when he found that his spray gun refused to work on the new hospital block. He was using white not red paint, and working in Pimlico.

Since then we've had a fair number of complaints and I can't seem to locate where the problem lies.

Perhaps you can help.

Joe Davis
(London Area Supervisor)

Note

Based upon a brief reference to such a case in *The Rational Manager,* by C. H. Kepner and B. B. Tregoe, this exercise was devised by Miss Elizabeth Andrews of the Industrial Society.

NOTES AND BIBLIOGRAPHY

Chapter 1. *The Nature of Thinking*
1. R. Thompson, *The Psychology of Thinking*, Penguin, 1959, p. 27.
2. For example, T. Dobzhansky in *The Biology of Ultimate Concern*, New American Library, 1967 : 'Man transcends all other life because he is, for the first time, life aware of itself (p. 68).
3. I. P. Pavlov, 'Bequest to Academic Youth', *Science*, Vol. 83 (1936), p. 369.
4. For such value-judgements in the definition of creativity, see (for example) *The Creative Organization*, ed. G. A. Steiner, Chicago and London, University of Chicago, 1965, p. 83; J. W. Haefele, *Creativity and Innovation*, New York, Reinhold; London, Chapman and Hall, 1965, p. 6.
5. *Op. cit.*, p. 41.
6. Tractatus Logico-Philosophicus (English translation, 1922), Prop. 4121.
7. C. S. Lewis, *Surprised by Joy*, Geoffrey Bles, 1955, pp. 206–7.
8. From William Blake's poem, *Eternity*.
9. Especially *A Life of One's Own*, Penguin, 1952 (written under the pseudonym Joanna Field).
10. Helmut de Terra, *Memories of Teilhard de Chardin*, Collins, 1964, p. 67. Cp. the remark about Newton by a contemporary 'Sir Isaac in mathematics, could sometimes see almost by intuition, even without demonstration .... And when he did propose conjectures in natural philosophy, he almost always knew them to be true at the same time', quoted in E. N. Da Costa Andrade, *Isaac Newton*, Max Parrish, 1950, p. 107.
11. J. Hadamard, *The Psychology of Invention in the Mathematical Field*, Dover, 1945.
12. Preface to Max Planck, *Where is Science Going?* trans. J. Murphy, Allen and Unwin, 1933.

13. J. Burnaby, *Amor Dei:* Hodder and Stoughton, 1938, p. 154.

Chapter 2. *Thinkers in Action*

T. E. LAWRENCE
From *The Seven Pillars of Wisdom,* Jonathan Cape, 1935, pp. 188–96.

GENERAL DWIGHT D. EISENHOWER
From *Crusade in Europe,* Heinemann, 1948, pp. 270–71.

SIR LAWRENCE BRAGG
From 'Fifty Years a Winner : A Profile of Sir Lawrence Bragg', BBC television, 2 December 1965; and a letter to *The Times* in November 1968.

C. S. FORESTER
From *Long Before Forty,* Michael Joseph, 1967, pp. 240–41.

Chapter 3. *Decision making*

1. From 'Life at the Top', The *Observer,* 24 May 1970.
2. *Ibid.*
3. Albert Speer, *Inside the Third Reich,* Weidenfeld and Nicolson, 1970, p. 100.
4. P. Drucker, *The Effective Executive,* Heinemann, 1967, p. 124.
5. P. Drucker, *The Practice of Management,* Heinemann, 1955, p. 355.
6. Reported in *The Times Business News,* 29 November 1968.
7. S. Weil, *Waiting on God,* Routledge and Kegan Paul, 1951, p. 56.
8. Lewis Carroll, *Through the Looking Glass* (1871), London, Dent, 1954, p. 224.
9. Robert L. Thorndike, 'How Children Learn the Principles and Techniques of Problem Solving', National Society for the Study of Education, *Forty-ninth Yearbook, Part 1,* Chicago, University of Chicago Press, 1950, p. 196.
10. Nicholas G. Nicolaidis, *Policy-Decision and Organization Theory,* Los Angeles, USC Bookstore, John W. Donner Memorial Fund Publication No. 11, 1960. This study was summarized and enlarged by John M. Pfiffner in his article, 'Administrative Rationality', *Public Administration Review,* Vol. 22, Summer, 1960, pp. 125–32.
11. P. Drucker, *The Effective Executive,* Heinemann, 1967, p. 113.

Chapter 4. *Sharing Decisions*
1. R. Tannenbaum and W. H. Schmidt, 'How to Choose a Leadership Pattern', *Harvard Business Review*, March-April 1958.
2. See J. Humble, *Management by Objectives in Action*, McGraw-Hill, 1970. For studies of participation in decision making see: K. Lewin, 'Group Decision and Social Change', in T. M. Newcomb and E. L. Hartley, *Readings in Social Psychology*, New York, Henry Holt & Co., 1947; J. Levine and J. Butler, 'Lectures on Group Decision in Changing Behavior', *Journal of Applied Psychology*, No. 36, 1952, pp. 29–33; E. B. Bennett, 'Discussions, Decision, Commitments and Consensus in Group Discussion', *Human Relations,* Vol. 8, 1955, pp. 251–73. For the beneficial effects of shared decision making when changes were to be introduced on a shop-floor, see L. Coch and J. R. P. French, 'Overcoming Resistance to Change', *Human Relations*, Vol. 1, 1948, pp. 512–32.
3. P. Gordon Walker, *The Cabinet*, Cape, 1970.
4. Yet even the President of the USA is subject to limitations in making decisions. For a discussion of five such limitations, see Theodore C. Sorenson, *Decision-Making in the White House*, Columbia University Press, 1964.
5. D. McGregor, *The Human Side of Enterprise*, New York, McGraw Hill, 1960.
6. N. R. F. Maier, *Problem-Solving Discussions and Conferences: Leadership Methods and Skills*, New York, McGraw-Hill, 1963.
7. The American behavioural scientist Rensis Likert seems to carry the concept of group acceptance to an extreme. He believes that group discussion is the best and only valid way to reach a good decision, that data gathering and integrating should be done by the group, and that decision making is the selection of a course of action by acclamation. See R. Likert, *New Patterns in Management,* New York, McGraw-Hill, 1957.
8. P. J. Sadler, *Leadership Style, Confidence in Management and Job Satisfaction*, Ashridge Management College Papers in Management Studies.
9. *Leadership and Motivation. Essays of Douglas McGregor,* ed. W. G. Bennis and E. H. Schein, Cambridge, Mass. and London, The MIT Press, 1966, p. 123. For a discussion relevant to this passage, see J. Adair, *Training for Leadership*, Macdonald, 1968, pp. 121–5.

10. For further information about suggestions schemes in Britain : The National Suggestion Schemes Association, 47 Elmcroft Avenue, Sidcup, Kent.

Chapter 5 : *Problem Solving*
1. G. Martineau, *Napoleon's St Helena* (translated from the French by F. Partridge), Murray, 1968, p. 47.
2. See K. Duncker, *On Problem Solving* (translated Lynnes Lees). Psychological Monographs, No. 270, 1945. See also his article : 'A Qualitative (Experimental and Theoretical) Study of Productive Thinking (Solving of Comprehensible Problems)', *Journal of Genetic Psychology*, 1926, Vol. 33, pp. 642–708.
3. *Ibid.*, pp. 108–9.
4. *Ibid.*, p. 24.
5. R. E. Adamson and D. W. Taylor, 'Functional fixedness as related to elapsed time and set', *J. Exp. Psychology*, 47, pp. 122–6.
6. L. Hudson, *Contrary Imaginations*, Methuen, 1966.
7. For an early formulation of the phases, see J. Dewey, *How We Think*, Boston, D. C. Heath, 1933.

Chapter 6. *Creative Thinking*
1. J. W. Haefele, *Creativity and Innovation*, New York, Reinhold; London, Chapman and Hall, 1962, p. 261.
2. J. Field, *A Life of One's Own*, Penguin Books, 1952, p. 87.
3. *Ibid.*, p. 94.
4. *Ibid.*, p. 100.
5. *Ibid.*, p. 128.
6. Reported in *The Times*, 20 February 1970
7. Book review published in *The Sunday Times*, May 1968.
8. J. D. Watson, *The Double Helix*, Weidenfeld and Nicolson, 1968.
9. K. Seelig, *Albert Einstein*, Zurich, Europa Verlag, 1954.
10. E. N. Da Costa Andrade, *Isaac Newton*, Max Parrish, 1950, p. 102.
11. R. Butler, *Creative Development*, Routledge and Kegan Paul, 1962, pp. 72–3.

Further Reading:
J. L. Lowes, *The Road to Xanadu*, New York, Houghton Mifflin, 1940. This is a classic study of the origins of Samuel Taylor

Coleridge's poem *Kubla Khan*. It shows that the main images in the poem had been dropped into 'the deep well' of his mind by the poet long before the famous dream in which he conceived it as a whole.

A. Koestler, *The Act of Creation* (London, Hutchinson, 1964). In this large tome (708 pages) Koestler introduced the term 'bisociation' in order to make a 'distinction between the routine skills of thinking on a single plane, as it were and the creative act, which ... always operates on more than one plane' (p. 35).

W. I. B. Beveridge, *The Art of Scientific Investigation*, (Revised edition, New York, Norton, 1957). Professor Beveridge wrote his book mainly as a guide to research students. He was Professor of Animal Pathology in the University of Cambridge. In an appendix (pp. 160–66), the author gives seventeen examples of scientists noticing and using 'chance' occurrences.

Creativity, ed. P. E. Vernon, Penguin Books, 1970. A representative and easily available collection of readings on the limited psychological research into the subject. It is divided into six parts: Pioneer Empirical Studies; Introspective Materials (including an excerpt from Henri Poincaré's classic account of his creative processes as a mathematician); Theoretical Contributions; Psychometric Approaches; Personality Studies; and Stimulating Creativity.

SOME EXPERIMENTAL INVESTIGATIONS INTO CREATIVITY

Relatively little experimental work has been carried out by psychologists. In 1969 Professor John Cohen of Manchester University's Department of Psychology remarked in a letter to the author: 'All in all, I don't think that creativity is a subject about which a great deal is known to scientists. I imagine that poets and artists have more understanding of what it is all about.' The following examples of sparse material are grouped according to the main research method employed.

1. Analysis of questionnaires filled in by particular groups:

Musicians. J. Bahle, 'Eindfall und Inspiration in Musikalischen Chaffen'. The reference to (and discussion of) this article may be found in J. W. Haefele, *op. cit.*, pp. 221–2, 277.

Mathematics. J. Hadamard, *The Psychology of Invention in the Mathematical Field*, Princeton University Press, 1945.

Inventors. J. Rossman, *The Psychology of the Inventor*, Washington, Inventor's Publishing Library, 1931.

Scientists. R. B. Cattell and J. E. Drerdahl, 'A Comparison of the Personality Profile (16PF) of Eminent Researchers with that of Eminent Teachers and Administrators, and of the General Population', *British Journal of Psychology*, Vol. 46, 1955.
W. Platt and R. A. Baker, 'The Relation of the Scientific Hunch to Research', *American Journal of Chemical Education*, Vol. 8, 1931.
C. W. Taylor and R. L. Ellison, 'Predicting Creative Performance from Multiple Measures', in *Widening Horizons in Creativity*, ed. C. W. Taylor, Wiley, 1964. Exerpts from it appear in *Creativity*, ed. P. E. Vernon.
2. Creators 'thinking aloud' while at work :
C. Patrick, *What is Creative Thinking?* New York, Philosophical Library, 1955.
W. E. Vinacke, *The Psychology of Thinking*, McGraw-Hill, 1952.
3. Deductions from creativity tests given to the general public :
J. P. Guildford, 'Traits of Creativity', in *Creativity and Its Cultivation,* ed. H. H. Anderson, New York, Harper, 1959.
J. W. Getzels and P. W. Jackson, *Creativity and Intelligence*, London, Wiley, 1962. See also Sir Cyril Burt's critical review of it in the *British Journal of Educational Psychology*, Nov., Vol. 32, 1962. Both are reprinted in *Creativity*, ed. P. E. Vernon, with other excerpts illustrating later research along these lines.
4. Psychological tests given to outstanding individuals :
Three articles by Anne Roe : 'A Psychological Study of Physical Scientists', *Genetical Psychology Monograph*, No. 43, 1951. 'A Psychologist Examines Sixty-Four Eminent Scientists', *Scientific American*, Vol. 187, 1952. Reprinted in *Creativity*, ed. P. E. Vernon. 'A Psychological Study of Biological Scientists', *Psychological Monograph*, No. 331, 1955. See also A. Roe, *The Making of a Scientist*, Dodd Mead, 1952.
5. Some current research projects :
Princeton University has a special laboratory investigating creativity. Sam Glucksberg, head of the research group, described its approach in *Think*, March-April 1968, the journal of IBM (USA).
Research into creativity is in progress at the Institute for Personality Assessment and Research in the University of California. The Director, Professor Donald W. Mackinnon, wrote articles on its work in *Productive Thinking in Education* (Washington, National Education Association, 1965) and *Personnel Administration,*

January-February 1968. Excerpts from his own research article, 'The Personality Correlates of Creativity: A Study of American Architects', first published in *Proceedings of the Fourteenth Congress on Applied Psychology*, Vol. 2, Munksgaard, 1962, have recently been reprinted in *Creativity*, ed. P. E. Vernon.

Chapter 7. *Decisions About People*
1. The *Observer*, 24 May 1970
2. See J. Adair, *Training for Leadership*, Macdonald, 1968, Chapter 1; cp. V. Packard, *The Pyramid Climbers*, Pelican Books, 1965.
3. William H. Whyte Jr, *The Organization Man*, New York, Simon & Schuster, 1955; London, Jonathan Cape, 1957.
4. B. Babington Smith, 'Systematic Observation', *Manpower and Applied Psychology*, Vol. 1, No. 2, 1967.
5. For a stimulating but speculative thesis that observation and analysis of a person's posture and gesture within specified limits will reveal basic natural qualities, see W. Lamb and D. Turner, *Management Behaviour*, London, Gerald Duckworth, 1970.
6. *IPM Digest*, Institute of Personnel Management, No. 65, November 1970.
7. P. Drucker, *The Effective Executive*, Heinemann, 1967, p. 26.
8. J. Adair, *Roundhead General*, Macdonald, 1969, p. 180.
   For further reading on interviewing as a specialized aspect of judging people, see: E. Sidney and M. Brown, *The Skills of Interviewing*, Tavistock, 1959. J. M. Fraser, *A Handbook of Employment Interviewing*, Macdonald and Evans, 2nd edn., 1966.

Chapter 8. *Experiments in Training*
SYNECTICS
1. W. J. J. Gordon, *Synectics: The Development of Creative Capacity*, Harper and Row, 1961.
2. *Ibid.*, p. 140.
BRAINSTORMING
3. A. F. Osborn, *Applied Imagination*, New York, Charles Scribner, 1953. See also C. H. Clark, *Brainstorming*, Doubleday, 1955, which contains the transcript of a brainstorming session.
4. *Ibid.*, pp. 300–301.
5. *Ibid.*, p. 297.

6. A. Meadow and S. J. Parnes, 'Evaluation of Training in Creative Problem Solving', *Journal of Applied Psychology*, 1959, pp. 189–94; E. Weisskopf-Joelson and T. S. Eliseo, 'An Experimental Study of the Effectiveness of Brainstorming', *Journal of Applied Psychology*, 1961, pp. 45–9.

7. D. W. Taylor, P. C. Berry and C. H. Block, 'Does Group Participation When Using Brainstorming Facilitate or Inhibit Creating Thinking?', *Administrative Science Quarterly*, 1958, pp. 23–47.

8. J. W. Haefele, *op. cit.*, p. 57.

9. *Problem-Solving: Research, Method, and Theory*, ed. B. Kleinmuntz, Wiley, 1966, p. 16.

10. S. J. Parnes, 'Education and Creativity', *Teachers College Record*, Vol. 64, 1963. Reprinted in *Creativity*, ed. P. E. Vernon, Penguin Books, 1970.

DR ABERCROMBIE

11. M. L. Johnson Abercrombie, *The Anatomy of Judgement: An Investigation into the Processes of Perception and Reasoning*, Penguin, 1969, p. 15.

12. *Ibid.*, p. 14.

13. *Ibid.*, p. 174.

14. *Ibid.*, p. 75.

15. *Ibid.*, p. 155.

KEPNER AND TREGOE

16. C. H. Kepner and B. B. Tregoe, *The Rational Manager: A Systematic Approach to Problem Solving and Decision Making*, New York, McGraw-Hill, 1965, pp. 44–6.

17. *Ibid.*, p. 17.

18. *Ibid.*, pp. 45–6.

19. *Ibid.*, p. 230.

20. *Ibid.*, p. 236.

21. For a brief description of the training, see 'The KT decision', *Business Management*, January 1969.

EDWARD DE BONO

22. The first three were originally published by Jonathan Cape, the fourth by Ward Lock.

23. *The Mechanism of Mind*, p. 257.

24. *Financial Times*, 23 October 1968.

25. *The Mechanism of Mind*, p. 275.

26. *The Uses of Lateral Thinking*, pp. 83, 90–91.

27. *Ibid.*, p. 147.

Chapter 9. *Training for Decisions*

1. Cp. Sir Frederick Bartlett, late Professor of Experimental
Psychology at Cambridge University : 'whenever the mind comes
into operation, most unmistakably it is by filling up gaps that
are left in the evidence that has been gained by direct observation', and 'thinking is essentially the filling up of gaps', from
The Mind at Work and Play (London, George Allen and
Unwin, 1955), pp. 121, 141. See also his book *Thinking* (same
publisher, 1958).
1958).
2. See J. Adair, *Training for Leadership,* Macdonald, 1968; A.
Adamson, *The Effective Leader*, Pitman, 1970.
3. For accounts of some prelimary research and contemporary
thinking on the part played by values in managerial thinking see
Industry and Values, ed. M. Ivens, Harrap, 1970, especially
Professor R. W. Revans's contribution, 'Values and Enterprise as
a Subject for Research', pp. 191–200.

Films:
Twelve Angry Men (1955). Lasts 96 minutes, and can be hired in
the United Kingdom from Film Distributor Association, 37/41
Mortimer St, London, W.1.
Critical Path (1963). Can be hired from the Central Film Library.

Conclusion
1. *Genesis,* Chapter 30, verse 26.
2. S. T. Coleridge, *Biographia Literaria,* ed. J. Shawcross, (Oxford,
Clarendon, 1970), Vol. 1. p. 85.

INDEX

Abercrombie, M. L. Johnson, 115, 117, 127, 128; quoted, 116, 118; Abercrombie method for creative thinking: content, 115–16; evaluation, 117–18; history, 115; methods of training, 117

Analysing, 15–16, 25; analysis defined, 15; depth mind in, 22, 23; in choosing personnel, 102, 105; in establishing aims, 54; pleasure behind, 16

Andrews, Elizabeth, 11, 153

Archimedes, 16

Aswan Dam, 62

Babington Smith, Bernard, 11; quoted, 103–4

Beagle, HMS, 98

Blake, William, 21

Bono, Edward de, 121, 122, 123, 124; quoted, 122–3

Bosticco, Mary, 76

Bradley, Omar, 35

Bragg, Lady, 43–4, 46

Bragg, Sir Lawrence, FRS, 11, 26, 40, 94, 98; BBC programme quoted, 40–47; his work, 40, 42; love of children, 43–4; views on science and moral values, 47–8

Brainstorming, 135; content, 112–13; evaluation, 113–15; history, 112; methods of training, 113

British Institute of Management, 113

Brown, Lady Margaret, 11

Buffalo, University of, 115

Butler, Reg, 98

California, University of, 96

Carroll, Lewis, 24, 62

Chardin, Teilhard de, 23

Charles-Edwards, David, 11

Churchill, Winston, 105

Clausewitz, Karl von, 27

Cohen, John, 11

Cole, Lord, 75; quoted, 75

Contraceptive pill, invention of, 96

Creative thinkers, types of, 99

Crick, Francis, 40, 96; on Sir Lawrence Bragg, 40, 44

Critical Path (film), 132

Critical Path Method, 142–3

Cromwell, Oliver, 107

Darwin, Charles, 98

Decision: about people, 101–8; acceptance and, 71–2; defined, 49–50; leadership decisions, 50–51; sharing, 65–6, 72–3, 74, 137; time factor in, 70; unforeseen consequences of, 62

Decision making, 51–62; consistency important in, 73; continuum, 66–8, 90, 137; courses open in, 56–8; creativity in, 75–8; democracy or authority in, 73, 74; implementing the decision, 58–60; making the decision, 60–62; models for, 62–4, 126–9; 'people dimension' in, 71, 73, 136–7; 'point of no return' in, 61, 132; problem solving and, 81–2; reviewing the factors, 55–6; specifying the aim, 52–5; subordinates in, 69; training for, 109–38; Whitbreads' course on, 131–2

Decision trees, 146

Depth mind dimension, 21–4, 52,

140; C. S. Forester on, 37–40; judgements about people and, 107; Marion Miller on, 91–3; R. L. Stevenson on, 94; 'sleeping on it', 59
Dewey, John, 101
Diabetes, 95
DNA molecule, 40, 44; thinking behind discovery of structure, 96–7
Dobzhansky, Theodosius, 17
Drawford, C. C., 76
Drucker, Peter, 63; quoted, 57, 58, 64, 107
Dudeney, A. E., 149
Duncker, Karl, 149; on problem solving, 83–5, 88

Einstein, Albert, 23, 99; quoted, 97–8
Eisenhower, Dwight D., 26; death of, 37; his decisions before D-Day, 33–7, 132
Electric dynamo, invention of, 95
Electron microscope, invention of, 96
Emotions: as dimension in thinking 92, 97, 100; in motivation towards problem solving, 87–8; values influencing, 20–21, 88
Everest, Mount, 141
Eysenck, H. J., 106

Faraday, Michael, 95
Field, Joanna, see Miller, Marion
Fleming, Sir Alexander, 95
Fonda, Henry, 136
Ford Motor Company: rewards for workers at, 77
Forester, C. S., 26, 94, 99; on depth mind and creativity, 37–40
Freud, Sigmund, 21

Games theory, 146–7

Gardner, Martin, 149
Gaulle, Charles de, 105
General Electric Company, 59
General Telephone and Electronics Company, 77
Gordon, William J. J., 109, 110, 112, 124
Guest, Keen and Nettlefolds Ltd, operational research at, 144–5

Haefele, J. W., 91, 114
Hadamard, J., 23
Harvard Business Review, 65, 70, 85
Harvard Business School, 128
Hejaz, the, 28, 33n
Heuristics, defined, 85
Hitler, Adolf, 57
Hodkin, Dorothy, 42–3
Hour-glass model of thinking contexts, 126–9
Hudson, Liam, 11

Illinois Institute of Technology, 95, 96
Industrial Society, 76, 137, 153
Institute of Personnel Management, 106
Integrity, defined, 104
Intuition, 22–3
Inventions: chance, 95; from pure research, 95–6

Jenner, 100
Jesus of Nazareth, 106
Johns-Manville Company, 109
Journal of the Association of Teachers of Management, 144
Judgement, defined, 115

Kant, 20
Kekulé, 26
Kendrew, Dr, 45, 47
Kepner, Charles H., 118, 119

Kepner-Tregoe Ltd, 11
Kepner-Tregoe method for decision making: content, 119–20; evaluation, 121; history, 118–19; methods of training, 120–21
Kimberley-Clark Company, 109

Lateral Thinking: content, 122–3; evaluation, 123–4; history, 121–2; methods of training, 123
Laue, M. T. F. von, 42, 47
Lawrence, T. E., 26; envisages guerrilla warfare, 30–31; thinking on the desert campaign, 27–33
Leach, Edmund, 47
Leigh-Mallory, Air Chief Marshal, 132; doubts about airborne invasion, 33–4, 35
Lewis, C. S., 21
Lincoln, Abraham, 69
Little, Arthur D., Inc., 109

McGregor, Douglas, 70, 74; on decision making, 74–5
Maier, Norman R. F., 71, 72
Management, as leadership, 50, 53, 136
Manager, the: his own values, 68–9; his ways of decision making, 66–8; techniques for, 142–7; Whitbreads' training course for, 130–37
Marquandt Aircraft Corporation, 77
Matrix isolation, discovery of, 96
Mattel Inc., 77
Maugham, W. Somerset, 98
Mecca, 27
Medina, 27
Miller, Marion, 22, 94; on thinking, 91–3
Mind, unconscious, see Depth mind dimension
Monowski, Prof., 95

Models, decision-making, 62–4; hour-glass, 126–9
Montgomery, Bernard, 36
Morgan Crucible Ltd, 77
Mozart, 100

Napoleon, 32; as decision maker, 80–81
National Science Foundation of America, 95
Network analysis, 142–3
Newton, Sir Isaac, 98, 130
Nicolaidis, Nicholas G., 63, 64
Nixon, Richard M., 37
Normandy invasion, 34–5; Utah Beach, 34, 35; weather preceding, 36–7

Oersted, H. C., 95
Operational Research, 143–6; at GKN, 144–5; queuing problems, 143
Osborn, Alexander, 112

Pasteur, Louis, 26, 94
Pauling, L. C., 44
Pavlov, I. P., 16
Penicillin, discovery of, 95
People, decisions about, 101–8; first impressions, 105–6
Perutz, Max, 45, 47
Plato, 30
Poincaré, J. H., 26
Preference theory, see Decision trees
Problem solving, 14, 79–81, 133–4; concepts used in, 88–90; decision making and, 81–2; exercise – the paint spray gun, 150–52; experience and, 87; motivation and, 87–8; phases of, 85–6; research into, 82–5; techniques for, 142–7; training for, 109–38
Problems: defined, 14, 79; 'functional fixedness', 84

Programme Evaluation and Review, 142-3
Purpose, in the abstract, 52, 53

RAC-Whirlpool Company, 109
Ramsay, Admiral, 36
RAND Corporation, California, 118
Rhodes, Jerry, 11
Ridgway, Gen., 35
Rockefeller Foundation, 115
Ruger, A., on problem solving, 82-3

St Augustine of Hippo, 24
St Peter, 106
Sandhurst, Royal Military Academy, 118
Saxe, Marshal, 32
Schmidt, Warren H., 65, 68, 70, 72, 78, 137
Scudder Food Products Inc.: account of suggestions scheme at, 76-7
Sherpa Tensing, 141
Shorter Oxford English Dictionary, 14, 15, 49, 85, 104, 129
Singer Sewing Machine Co., 109
Slim, Lord, 104
Sloan, Albert P., 57
Smallpox, discovery of vaccination against, 100
Smuts, J. C., 23
Solving, defined, 14
Sourian, 124
Speer, Albert, 57
Spurrell, D. J., 144
Stagg, J. M., 35, 36
Stevenson, Robert Louis, on creativity, 94
Stryker, Perrin, 121
Suggestions schemes, 76-8
Synectics: content, 109-11; evaluation, 111-12; history, 109; methods of training, 111

Synthesizing, 16-18, 25, 136; depth mind in, 22; in choosing personnel, 103, 105; in establishing aims, 54; synthesis defined, 16

Tannenbaum, Robert, 65, 68, 70, 72, 78, 137
Tedder, Air Chief Marshal, 36
Thinking: creative, 90-100, 123-4; derivation from Latin, 16; emotion as dimension in, 92, 97, 100; evolution and, 14-15; hour-glass model, 126-9; Marion Miller on, 91-3; nature of, 13-14, 25, 64; Simone Weil on, 59-60; Whitbreads Ltd, 131, 135-6
Thompson, Robert, 14
Thomson, Sir George, 45-6
Thomson, J. J., 42
Times, The, 47, 76
Training: aim of, 130; theory and practice, 129-30
Tregoe, Benjamin B., 118, 119
Turkish army, Lawrence assesses, 29
Twelve Angry Men (film), 136

Unilever company, 50, 75
University College, London, 115

Valuing, 18-21, 25; depth mind in, 22, 24; in choosing personnel, 105; in establishing aims, 55; moral values, 19
Video tape, invention of, 95-6
Virco, Dr, 42
Von der Goltz, 27-8, 30
Von Mering, Prof., 95
Von Moltke, Helmuth C. B., Baron, 57
Waddington, C. H., on thinking behind discovery of structure of DNA, 96-7
Wadi Ais, Arabia, 27

Waller, Sir William, on Cromwell, 107
Waterloo, Battle of, 81
Watson, James, 40, 96, 97
Webster's Dictionary, 115
Weil, Simone, on thinking, 59–60
Weinstock, Sir Arnold, 59
Wejh, Arabia, 27
Wertheimer, Max, 83, 88
Westwood, Barry, 41–7 passim

Whitbreads Ltd, training course at, 130–37
Wilson, C. T. R., 42
Woodroofe, Ernest, 50, 53; quoted, 51, 53, 101

Xenophon, 31
X-ray crystallography, 40, 41

Yenbo, Arabia, 27